Walter Armstrong

Wrestliana, or the History of the Cumberland & Westmoreland

Wrestling Society in London

Since the Year 1824

Walter Armstrong

Wrestliana, or the History of the Cumberland & Westmoreland Wrestling Society in London
Since the Year 1824

ISBN/EAN: 9783337204112

Printed in Europe, USA, Canada, Australia, Japan

Cover: Foto ©ninafisch / pixelio.de

More available books at **www.hansebooks.com**

WRESTLIANA;

OR, THE

𝕳istory of the Cumberland & Westmoreland

WRESTLING SOCIETY

IN LONDON

SINCE THE YEAR 1824.

BY

WALTER ARMSTRONG, Hon. Sec.

Then at lowpin' he'll gang a full yard owre them aw,
And at rustlin', whilk o' them dare try him a faw.
ROBERT ANDERSON.

Now, clear the ring ! for hand to hand
The manly wrestlers take their stand.
SIR WALTER SCOTT.

LONDON:
SIMPKIN, MARSHALL, & CO., STATIONERS' HALL COURT.

1870.

LONDON:
GEORGE BERRIDGE & CO., PRINTERS,
EASTCHEAP WORKS, E.C.

ADVERTISEMENT.

THIS volume contains a full account of all the transactions of the Cumberland and Westmoreland Wrestling Society in London since 1824, the annual gatherings at the Agricultural Hall and elsewhere, with remarks on most of the celebrated wrestlers who have figured therein; together with detailed lists of the winners, first, second, and third, up to the present time; the contributions to the charitable institutions of the two counties; and amounts given in prizes during the last ten years; the whole forming a complete history of the Cumberland and Westmoreland wrestling in the metropolis.

CONTENTS.

INTRODUCTION.

THE Cumberland and Westmoreland Wrestling Society was the first, and, till a recent period, the only one existing in the metropolis that had for its object the practice and annual celebration of athletic sports; and though in the present day the importance of athletic exercises in the promotion of health, and the due development of the physical powers, is becoming more acknowledged and appreciated, as shown in the establishment of Gymnasiums and Athletic Societies, both in London and elsewhere; yet, the above, as far as London itself is concerned, stands alone, both in point of influence, and the pre-eminent skill and science displayed in the performance of the particular exercises practised by its members.

The origin of this Society, and the exact date of its establishment is somewhat uncertain; the best living authorities, however—very old members—agree that it has existed more than a century, the earliest mention of its annual gatherings being, that the natives of Cumberland and Westmoreland were in the habit of meeting on Kennington Common on Good Friday to celebrate their favourite sports of wrestling and leaping. The prizes competed for in these days were insignificant in value, and few in number, a belt being awarded to the champion of the wrestling arena, to which all weights were admitted, and a pair of buckskin gloves to the best leaper, in imitation of the prizes at that time given for competition in many parts of Cumberland and Westmoreland.

The local affections and kindly feelings towards each other, so strongly characteristic of the natives of these counties, not only kept alive their ardour, but lent increased attraction to their meetings, drawing together a large number of old friends, many of them old playmates and school-fellows, who, since leaving their northern homes, and being occupied in various pursuits in different parts of London, seldom met, except on such occasions, and at no time to enjoy themselves so much.

As years flew by, and its numbers increased, the Society gradually became more organized; better, and a greater number, of prizes were given for competition, till, in the year 1824, we find the first record of a code of rules, and a regular staff of officers appointed to carry out the sports and conduct the business of the Society. Gradually, although at first confined to wrestling—irrespective of weights—and leaping, the competition has been extended, and prizes given for other sports, such as pole jumping, hurdle racing, etc. Competitors have also, under certain restrictions, and by permission of the Committee, been allowed to come from the north to contend for certain classes of prizes, though debarred from others reserved for the London residents only.

Since the commencement the annual meetings have been held in various places :—viz., Kennington Common, Chelsea, St. John's Wood, Chalk Farm, Highbury Barn, Copenhagen House, Hornsey Wood House, Hackney Wick, and for the last six years at the Agricultural Hall, Islington, a place admirably adapted for so large an assemblage. In consequence of the unparalleled success which has attended the meetings held at the last-named place, the Society is now in a flourishing condition. Having passed through all the dangers which more than once imperilled its very existence, its now firm basis may be said to rest in a measure on the valued permission of Sir Richard Mayne for the wrestling to take place on Good Friday. After a full explanation was given of the nature and objects of the Society—combining charity with manly exercise—the worthy Chief Commissioner never hesitated a moment to sanction the meeting on the day named above, and at the same time gave instructions that as many men as might be required for the purpose of keeping order would be placed at the service of the Society.

In the year 1845, at the suggestion of Mr. Margetson, the old practice of collecting the funds in subscriptions of two shillings and sixpence—that amount, as now, creating a member—was discontinued in favour of hiring the ground on Good Friday and taking the entrance money. The success of the alteration has been of late years assisted by the growing taste for athletic sports; the prizes offered for competition have been considerably increased in value, and the charitable institutions of the two counties have been proportionately benefited. Up to the present time the donations handed to these benevolent associations have reached the amount of four hundred guineas. Great credit is due to Mr. Margetson for the persevering manner in which he has stuck to the Society through all its vicissitudes during a period of over forty years. But for his wise counsels, the dangers which so frequently menaced the well-being of the Institution might have proved fatal. A wrestler himself in his younger days— and one of the very best at his weight (11 stone) —before he was twenty years of age he had thirty belts hanging up in his father's house in Westmoreland. Mr. Margetson had the honour of winning a belt at the Ferry sports at Windermere, when Professor Wilson was present amongst the spectators. The grand old Professor shook hands with him in the presence of the assembled multitude, and pronounced him the best wrestler in England, at the same time offering to back him to wrestle any man of his weight who could be produced.

Professor Wilson was a great athlete, and in these days used to wrestle the champion at the conclusion of the sports held in the neighbourhood of the Lakes which he invariably attended.

Of late years Mr. Margetson has left much of the management of the business of the Society to its younger members; it may be mentioned that before relaxing his energies as an effective member, he was successful in securing the Agricultural Hall for the Good Friday of 1864, and where the sports have been held ever since. It may not be amiss to state here that amongst the younger members, the most prominent is Mr. Thomas Mein, the Treasurer. Mr. Mein is on the shelf now as a wrestler, but in promoting the sports, and augmenting the funds, thereby swelling the donations to the benevolent institutions, he is shedding a lustre round his name which will far eclipse his former celebrity. During the intervals of his other duties, no man has worked harder for the Society than Mr. Mein. All honour to him for so doing, and long may he be spared to lend a helping hand to this deserving insti-

tution, and to assist in dispelling the idea prevalent
amongst that portion of the public which knows little
of wrestling, and its associations—viz., that the favourite sport of the natives of Cumberland and Westmoreland is brutal and debasing. This vague notion
exists to some extent amongst a certain few, but it
is a very grave mistake indeed; that there are now
a distinct race of professionals in the northern
counties who live by the exercise of their thews
and sinews is quite true, but at the same time,
it must be borne in mind, that this scientific
exercise is participated in by all classes on
the border. A great many of the athletes are the
sons of the landed proprietors, who have plenty of
leisure to enjoy these popular amusements, which are
of frequent occurrence in every valley, however re-
mote. The champion's belt, which is the great trophy
at these meetings, may be seen in almost every country house, suspended from the ceiling, sometimes to
the number of twenty or thirty, hanging in a row.
These trophies are regarded as treasured heirlooms,
and are worn as proudly, and won as honestly as the
ribbons and garters of more prominent statesmen.
Not only in all the towns, but in the most hidden
recesses of Cumberland and Westmoreland, these
belts are offered for competition; the magnificence of
the mountain scenery always lends a charm to the
place of meeting, the swelling hills looking down on

the beautiful spot chosen for the foreground of the picture; the smooth and grassy ring, filled with onlookers, whose knowledge of and interest in the sports unite in making these beautiful exercises very different indeed from the scenes of the prize ring or the race course. Perfect good humour always prevails amongst the competitors, who are amongst the most splendid specimens of suppleness, strength, and form that Britain boasts of. Charles Dickens once paid a visit to the ring at Windermere, and has thus described the wrestling in the pages of *Household Words* :—

" 'Nay, you're over weight, John, by two pounds,' says the clerk of the ring to some candidate seated in the weighing scale, who smiles good naturedly, and takes off nearly everything, but still is not quite qualified; he puts, therefore, a couple of great coats on, and takes a run in the road by the lake's side, whereby his too solid flesh being swelled and dissolved into a dew, he comes to scale a light weight after all. There are a great many 'lay-downs' in the first round, so that the wrestling gets select, and very much improves as it proceeds. The third round comprehends, therefore (unless in the case of some accidental defeat) a score of the best men. They strip to their drawers and flannel waistcoats, exhibiting such studies for the painter and the sculptor as are rarely seen elsewhere. They shake hands before commencing in token of amity; nor indeed in the thick and strain of the struggle, while the face of each is over the shoulder of the other, and every muscle is exerted to the utmost, do these fine fellows exhibit any trace of savageness or personal animosity.

"Two umpires, nestors of the wrestling ring, walk round the combatants, and observe them narrowly; nor is their decision ever impugned by the losing man. While the pair are taking hold, gratuitous advice is offered to them freely by their friends, who sit or stand around the ring, but when they grapple each other a perfect torrent of Bonnie Carels, or Bonnie Kendals, as the case may be, cleaves the air. Then they strive, then they strain shoulder to shoulder, neck to neck, and at last touch ground perhaps, so nearly at the same instant as to require the most practised eye to award the fall; or, whirling circularly as in Fakir-dance, are cast violently to earth apart, or one, across the victor's thigh, comes heels over head, and measures all his inches upon the green sward with a thud. This last fall is the only dangerous one, and that only in the case of very heavy weights, and of very indifferent performers. Good wrestlers very rarely hurt one another.

"This quiet looking giant by our side, who has been champion often and often, and will be so again this day, although he is nearly forty, and more than twelve

years past the wrestler's prime, has never, in his twenty
years' experience ever been hurt. He won his first
man's belt when a lad of sixteen years old, and in
his house, across the lake yonder—a clean, neat little
inn, set in a wilderness of flowers—has no less than
one hundred and seventy-four of these wrestling
zones; of all colors they are, and of all descriptions,
from the broad, plain, Manchester-looking belt, won
at the matter of fact and unornamental town, to the
splendid award of Newcastle, embossed with the
silver towers. Besides the mere leather (although
there is nothing like it), there is of course a
very considerable prize in money, averaging, perhaps,
twenty pounds. Lesser pecuniary rewards are proportionately distributed among the less successful combatants, and besides these, a subscription prize is
commonly made up by the stewards or spectators for
which the sixteen last standers wrestle over again.
Between the light and heavy weight matches (which
are generally on following days), there are all sorts
of other amusements, running matches, for a mile or
so, dog trails, jumping matches, for which not only
the aborigines enter, but usually several visitors,
University men, and the like, who reckoning upon the
iron shod boots and rough appearance of the natives
are surpised to find them, when stripped, as lithe
and active as themselves, and indeed a trifle more so!
They are of course a lighter set of men, for the most

part, than even the light weight wrestlers. There is
jingling also, a sport which consists of blind-folding
a number of men, and turning them out into the arena
which has previously been strewed with sacks full of
sawdust, to pursue some fleet-footed athlete, who
carries a bell. It is great fun to watch these unfor-
tunates taking accurate bearings of these sacks before
they are blind-folded, and then to see the pitiless
officials set these impediments totally afresh, besides
turning each performer three times round at the
commencement of the game. But the most graceful
of all the treats at the ferry, is the pole leaping, when
it is a candidate's last chance of three, his trial of
course becomes proportionally exciting; shouts of
encouragement greet him on all sides, and the women,
if he be a bonnie laddie, often shed tears in their
enthusiasm. The heavy weight wrestlers generally
close these amusements. If others were Apollos,
each of these is surely a Hercules; their grip is like
the hug of a bear. The champion here, who was so
good as to show us how to ' take hold,' the other
day, in his garden, has left his mark indelibly in our
back, besides having compressed our ribs so that we
cannot breathe right yet. It has come to the last
round, and our giant friend has but one foe to deal
with—a true son of Anak, as tall if not so big as
himself—he has got his work cut out for him, say the
old hands; but success has made him somewhat over

bold. How quietly he suffers these mighty arms to
be placed around him, and those strong fingers to feel
like one in the dark for a certain hold. Now they
have gripped at an advantage, and the foe is only
waiting for him to have hold likewise. He has hold!
He has hold! see how they grapple and strain.
'Bonnie Robson,' 'Bonnie Longmire,' so interested
this time in the individuals as to call them by their
own names instead of the localities from which they
come. Three to two on Longmire ; two to one, five
to——Longmire's down! Robson's felled him!
Bonnie Robson! And indeed it was so ; very quiet,
but very grim our giant looked. 'It is the best of
three for the last round,' quoth he as he took up
earth in his hands to prevent them slipping, remind-
ing us of the preparatory horn practice which the
bull indulges himself in on the turf before he charges.
This time it is two to one on Robson, who is indeed a
very good man, but he is felled nevertheless, and the
third time he is felled likewise, after a struggle such
as the old Greek gods were wont to delight in sitting
above the thunder on Olympus' top, or the Roman
Cæsars, little less divine, in that great wrestler's ring
by the Eternal City. So our giant friend has won
his one hundred and seventy-fifth girdle, and is champion after all."

In the celebrated Olympian games, the only reward
obtained by the conqueror was a crown of olive. The

games were celebrated every fifth year, and were continued for four successive days. These were the most ancient and most solemn of all the Greek festivals, and drew together not only the majority of the inhabitants of Greece, but also people from the neighbouring islands and countries. Indeed, so much importance was attached to them, that the period of their celebration became an era amongst the Greeks, who computed their time by it. The conquerors returned home in a chariot drawn by four horses, and to render the ceremony of their entrance into their native city more imposing, instead of going through the gates, a breach was made in the wall. Ten months exercise at the public gymnasium was necessary before a competitor was allowed to enter the lists, and the wrestlers were in the habit of anointing themselves with oil, to brace their limbs, and to render their bodies slippery.

Although running, leaping, boxing, and throwing the quoit were engaged in by the athletes, wrestling appears to have been the principal amusement. The wrestlers were appointed by lot. Some little balls, superscribed by a letter, were thrown into a silver urn ; those throwing the same letter had to contend with each other. It is said, that not only were ladies present as spectators, but also frequently amongst the competitors, and were sometimes rewarded with the crown. We are not told whether the crown was ever awarded to the fair ones for wrestling, indeed it is hardly likely, although in our day a parallel might be found. A good story is told of a lady who won the heavy weight prize at Haithwaite-yett, Nichol Forest; as, however, the truth of the matter is perhaps open to doubt, it would not be advisable to particularize.

Wrestling holds a high position amongst the bodily exercises of a great many countries, and in the encouragement of these sports, something more than mere pastime is kept in view. Like the ancient Greeks and Romans, these exercises are probably considered a fitting preparation for the exigences of war. It is much practised even in Japan. They hold their wrestling in the open air, in a ring surrounded by a railing about half the height of the spectators, who are as much excited by the performances as our own Cumberland and Westmoreland admirers of the sport. Their mode of wrestling is after the fashion of the Cornwall and Devon men. At the conclusion of the contests, each victor presents himself to the judge, who awards a prize of silver or gold plate, bearing the imperial arms.

There is a wrestler in Switzerland by name Halpenau, he is called the wrestler-king of the Canton Berne, and has a grasp like an iron vice; his mode of wrestling is to swing his opponents round his head, and but for their clinging to him, their fall would sometimes be no laughing matter. The canton

at present, however, has two wrestler-kings. The
name of the other is Wohlreich, a huge mountain of
a man, who might with truth be called the Swiss
Jameson. Though not so scientific as Halpenau, he
has more weight and strength, and can lift a man as
easily as ordinary mortals can carry a baby. Their
last contest was abandoned because neither could
obtain the victory, so that Berne contains two
wrestler-kings.

In Switzerland the wrestlers are carefully watched
by the committee, and fair felling is strictly enforced.
In the matter of science they are far inferior to our
own champions. Jameson or Wright would stand a good
chance of winning the long-wooled sheep there, which
is the prize in the Swiss wrestling ring. Jameson is,
undoubtedly, the most difficult man to throw of all
the champions of this generation; his enormous
bulk would have made him more than a match for
Longmire, although the latter, in point of science,
was his superior. Jackson, of Kennieside, the finest
wrestler of his day, might probably have held his
own with him, but no more. Wright is certainly
Jameson's equal in some respects, but labours under
the disadvantage of inferior weight. Noble Ewbank,
although a fine wrestler, was never equal to Jameson.
Richard Chapman, of Patterdale, figured in Jackson's
time. Chapman was a good wrestler, and won the
heavy weight prize at Carlisle three years in succes-

sion; his last year was 1841, when Jackson took up the game, and won the four succeeding years. William Roblaw, of Egremont; R. Gordon, of Plumpton; William Donald, of Dereham, are all distinguished names. R. Atkinson, the Sleagill giant, although no wrestler, had the credit (?) of crushing his opponents to the earth, and winning some prizes. About 1825 we have John Weightman, of Hayton. Weightman was a thorough athlete, and, as a wrestler, unsurpassed. He was seen walking through the streets of Carlisle some years ago (when he must have been quite sixty) with all the jauntiness of his youthful days. Weightman was soon recognized, . and the people were heard saying to each other, "There goes Weightman, of Hayton." His fame as a wrestler had lived forty years. Of late years, the two best light weight men have been John Palmer, of Bewcastle, and James Scott, of Carlisle. John Palmer's feat of winning the light and heavy weight prizes at Carlisle, in the same year, is without parallel. There was no getting him down. Scott, with the same tenacity of foothold, united all the graces of his art, and was the most scientific buttocker of modern times.

WRESTLIANA.

1824.

AT a numerous and respectable meeting of the natives of the counties of Cumberland and Westmoreland residing in London, held at the Admiral Duncan Tavern, Charing Cross, March 25th, 1824, Mr. John Goulding in the chair,

It was resolved :—

1st.—That a subscription be entered into for the purpose of procuring a silver cup, two silver snuff-boxes, and two gold seals, to be wrestled for, and a pair of gloves to be leapt for, on Good Friday, April 16, 1824.

2nd.—That each individual subscribe two shillings and sixpence or upwards, and that none but subscribers, natives of the two counties, be allowed to wrestle.

3rd.—That a cup be given to the best wrestler, a snuff-box to the second, and a gold seal to the third.

4th.—That the whole of the subscribers who have entered the ring for the first prizes be allowed to wrestle for the two last, viz., a silver snuff-box and a gold seal, except the winners of the three first prizes.

B

5th.—That any individual who gains the silver cup be ever after excluded.

' 6th.—That none be allowed to wrestle who have not resided in London, or within the Bills of Mortality, six months.

7th.—That the gloves be given to the best leaper at four hops and a leap.

8th.—That the whole of the subscribers' names, competitors, be put into a bag, and on the day of wrestling be drawn out one by one, that they wrestle first and second, third and fourth, and so on; that the first name be entered in the minute-book, and placed No. 1; the second drawn be entered the last number, and in like-manner till the whole are drawn out; that the conqueror's name be always written in the same line opposite to the person thrown, that after the first round they then be called together, first and last, and in case there should be an odd number at last, that then they toss up, and the odd man stand out; but if it appear one man has wrestled one round less than the other, then the two shall toss which wrestles him.

9th.—That the Stewards for the present year be Messrs. William Chambers, George Byers, Joseph Collins, John Sowerby, and Edward Lamb, and that the sole management of the wrestling be vested in them. That in case of a disputed fall, a majority of them shall decide, and any individual objecting to their decision shall have his name erased from the list.

10th.—That the Stewards be requested to provide the prizes, and submit them for the inspection of the subscribers the evening before the wrestling. That the second prize be one-half the value of the first, the third one-fifth less than the second, the fourth one-fourth less than the third, and the fifth one-third less than the fourth; and that the cup and snuff-boxes have suitable inscriptions.

11th.—That the Stewards be requested to order a supper at some convenient tavern, and that they name both the tavern and place of wrestling at least one week previous to Good Friday.

12th.—That the whole of the rules, together with the minutes of the proceedings, be entered in the book which shall hereafter be kept for that purpose.

JOHN GOULDING, *Chairman.*

The wrestling took place on Good Friday, April 14th. Nearly 200 competitors entered the ring, and, at the conclusion of the sports, the following gentlemen were declared the winners of the three prizes:—

First prize, a silver cup . . John Dobson
Second ditto, a silver snuff-box . J. Richardson
Third ditto, a gold seal . . William Graham

The gloves were won by James Johnson.

The following prizes were also wrestled for on Whit-Monday, June 7th, of the same year—viz., a

silver snuff-box; two gold seals; and two pounds
ten shillings.

Fourth Round.

Stood.	Fell.
E. Fisher	Jos. Brown
G. Byers	William Brown
Thomas Richardson	William Harrison
Jos. Rudd	Jos. Sowerby

Fifth Round.

G. Byers	J. Fisher
Thomas Richardson	Jos. Rudd

Final Fall.

G. Byers	Thos. Richardson

The prizes were awarded as below:—

First prize, a silver snuff-box	Geo. Byers
Second ditto, a gold seal	Thos. Richardson
Third ditto, a gold seal	Jos. Rudd
Fourth ditto, two pounds	E. Fisher
Fifth ditto, ten shillings	J. Brown

1825.

At a numerous meeting held on the 10th February,
1825, it was proposed and unanimously agreed that
a subscription should be entered into for the purpose
of carrying into effect the resolutions of the previous
year. Amendment to the eleventh resolution, "That
the Stewards name the place of wrestling and where
the supper shall be held one *month* previous to the
day appointed." The following gentlemen were
elected stewards:—

Mr. Geo. Byers
„ Jno. Martin
„ Thos. Richardson
„ Jos. Rudd
„ Richard Lamb

The wrestling was held on Good Friday, and, after a spirited and manly competition, reflecting the greatest credit upon the competitors, the winners of the different prizes were declared as below:—

FIRST TIME OVER.

First prize, silver cup . .	Jno. Beaty
Second ditto, silver snuff-box .	William Graham
Third ditto, silver snuff-box .	Jos. Lambert
Fourth ditto, gold seal . .	Jos. Rudd

SECOND TIME OVER.

First prize, silver snuff-box .	William Dent
Second ditto, silver snuff-box .	William Metcalf
Third ditto, gold seal . .	Jno. Cowing

The gloves were won by Stephen Fawcett.

1826.

A meeting was held on the 10th of February, 1826, for the purpose of making arrangements for carrying out the wrestling, and to take measures for raising subscriptions towards that object.

STEWARDS FOR THIS YEAR.

Mr. Joseph Bow
„ Henry Thompson
„ Joseph Bird
„ Mark Nicholson
„ John Watson

The wrestling was held on Good Friday. The winners of the prizes were

First prize, silver cup . . .	Robert Hall
Second ditto, silver snuff-box .	Jos. Dobson

The final wrestle between Hall and Dobson was a very unsatisfactory one, the referee ruled that Dobson had allowed himself to be unfairly thrown, therefore the prize which he would otherwise have received was withheld.

1827.

The subscribers to the Society met in great force at the "Admiral Duncan" Tavern, on Thursday, the 8th of February, 1827, to elect Stewards, and to take into consideration other matters connected with the wrestling. Great disapprobation was expressed at the conduct of Joseph Dobson in making a sham wrestle with Robert Hall the previous year. It was therefore proposed, seconded, and carried by a large majority, that Joseph Dobson be excluded from again entering the ring. The following gentlemen were then elected as Stewards :—

Mr. Jno. Goulding
  ,,   Atkinson Brunskill
  ,,   Joseph Rudd
  ,,   John Westmoreland
  ,,   Isaac Hinde

At a subsequent meeting held at the "Admiral Duncan" Tavern, Joseph Dobson, who was present, complained that the forgoing resolution had been passed in his absence. He requested that the sense of the meeting should be again taken on the subject. The question was fully discussed by those present, and the resolution confirmed by a large majority.

At a meeting held at the "Admiral Duncan" Tavern, on Thursday, the 15th of March, the following resolutions were agreed to :—

"That a Treasurer be appointed to receive from the Stewards every Thursday evening, all monies collected for the wrestling, and that the amounts and names of subscribers be entered in a book kept for that purpose."

It was then proposed, "That Mr. Jackson Stainton be appointed Treasurer," and carried unanimously.

The annual wrestling took place at Mr. Hintons' the "Eyre Arms" Tavern, St. John's Wood, on Good Friday, the 6th of April. The day was unusually fine, and about 1,000 persons assembled to witness the sports. Upwards of 170 competitors entered the ring. The wrestling commenced between one and two o'clock, and was kept up, with great spirit, till half-past seven in the evening. At the conclusion of the sports upwards of 200 gentlemen sat down to an excellent dinner, in the large room of the tavern, and, at the request of Mr. Graham, the champion of the day, Mr. Goulding, was called to the chair. Shortly after the cloth was removed the Chairman presented the prizes to the winners.

FIRST TIME OVER.

First prize, silver cup . .	Wm. Graham
Second ditto, gold snuff box .	John Ellwood.
Third ditto, silver snuff box .	Robert Winter

SECOND TIME OVER.

First prize, silver snuff box, . .	Wm. Mars
Second ditto, gold seal . . .	Wm. Fawcett
Third ditto, gold seal . . .	Joseph Stamper
Fourth ditto, gold seal . . .	Wm. Harrison

FIRST TIME OVER.

Sixth Round.

Stood.	Fell.
R. Winter	Tim Dobson
J. Ellwood	J. Atkinson
William Graham	William Fawcett

Seventh Round.

William Graham	R. Winter

J. Ellwood, odd man.

Final Fall.

William Graham	J. Ellwood

SECOND TIME OVER.

Fifth Round.

Stood.	Fell.
J. Stamper	J. Watson
William Fawcett	Jos. Steele
William Mars	William Harrison

Sixth Round.

William Fawcett	J. Stamper

William Mars, odd man.

Final Fall.

William Mars	William Fawcett

William Graham, the champion of the meeting, wrestled well throughout, and threw his men in a most scientific and graceful style. At the conclusion he was loudly and deservedly applauded. It may be remarked that his success here has followed him to another branch of sport; of late years, Mr. Graham has figured prominently in the racing world, and is now distinguished as the fortunate owner of the celebrated Formosa, the winner of the St. Leger and Oaks of 1868.

The following remarks are copied from *Bell's Life*, dated April 8th, 1827 :—" The first prize was won by William Graham, of Dufton Wood, near Appleby; he is only nineteen years of age, but possesses a most athletic frame and wonderful strength. In vain did his opponents try every art, by twisting their limbs round his, and bearing their whole weight upon his body, to throw him off his balance; he stood as if rooted to the earth, holding his antagonist in his arms until, watching his opportunity, he shook him off and dashed him to the ground. It may carry some notion of Mr. Graham's prowess to state that he never once came to the ground with his opponent, although, it seldom happens that any good wrestler can throw his man without falling on him."

1 8 2 8.

The following gentlemen were elected as Stewards for the Cumberland and Westmoreland Wrestling Society, at a meeting held at the " Admiral Duncan" Tavern, on Thursday, the 24th January, 1828.

Mr. William Graham
„ George Byers
„ John Atkinson
„ William Fawcett
„ John Harrison
Treasurer, Mr. Jackson Stainton

At a meeting held at the same place on the 13th March, it was agreed that Joseph Dobson should again be allowed to contend for the prizes offered by the Society ; having been debarred one year, being considered sufficient punishment for the offence alleged against him.

The annual wrestling took place at Mr. Hinton's, the " Eyre Arms" Tavern, St. John's Wood, on Good Friday, April the 4th. Nearly 3000 persons were present, and upwards of 200 competitors entered the ring.

After the wrestling, over 250 gentlemen sat down to dinner, which was served up in the best style of the worthy host. Mr. Goulding took the chair, at the request of the champion of the day (Mr. Percival).

After the substantial repast had received a due share of attention, the prizes were presented to the various winners by the Chairman, as follows :—

FIRST TIME OVER.

First prize, silver cup . . . William Percival
Second ditto, silver snuff box . Thomas Fawcett
Third ditto, silver snuff box .. Joseph Dobson
Fourth ditto, gold seal . . Christopher Halliday

SECOND TIME OVER.

First prize, silver snuff box . Philip Thompson
Second prize silver snuff box . John Atkinson
Third ditto, silver snuff box . William Robinson
Fourth ditto, gold seal . . James Richardson
Fifth ditto, gold seal . . . William Fawcett

The gloves were won by William Mossop.

FIRST TIME OVER.

Fifth Round.

Stood.	Fell.
C. Halliday	J. Ellwood
T. Fawcett	E. Dawson
J. Stamper	R. Sewell
William Percival	Tim. Dobson
Jos. Dobson	William Robinson

Sixth Round.

T. Fawcett	J. Stamper
William Percival	C. Holliday

Seventh Round.

William Percival	Jos. Dobson

T. Fawcett, odd man

Final Fall.

William Percival	T. Fawcett

SECOND TIME OVER.

Fourth Round.

Stood.	Fell.
P. Thompson	C. Gaddes
W. Fawcett	J. Rudd
J. Richardson	M. Dodd
William Robinson	J. Ellwood

Fifth Round.

P. Thompson	J. Richardson
John Atkinson	William Fawcett

William Robinson, odd man

Sixth Round.

Stood.   Fell.
P. Thompson   William Robinson
        J. Atkinson, odd man

Final Fall.

P. Thompson   J. Atkinson

1829.

The election of Stewards for this year took place at the "Admiral Duncan" Tavern, on Thursday, the 5th of February. Messrs. Joseph Rudd, Thomas Teasdale, William Harrison, Jacob Craig, and Robert Beck, were elected to carry out the sports; Mr. Jackson Stainton was appointed Treasurer. The sports took place on Good Friday. Subjoined is a return of the wrestling, commencing with the Fourth Round.

FIRST TIME OVER.

Fourth Round.

Joseph Wills	Jacob Craig
William Robinson	T. Fawcett
William Fenton	Joseph Stockdale
Joseph Stamper	James Johnson
E. Dawson	John Atkinson
W. Dennison	George Robinson
Joseph Dobson	M. Smith
J. Sewell	John Ellwood

Fifth Round.

Joseph Stamper	E. Dawson
J. Wills	W. Dennison
W. Robinson	Joseph Sewell
Joseph Dobson	William Fenton

Sixth Round,

Stood.	Fell.
Joseph Stamper	W. Robinson
Joseph Dobson	Joseph Wills

Seventh Round.

Joseph Dobson	Joseph Stamper

SECOND TIME OVER.

Third Round.

James Johnson	Thomas Temple
Joseph Slack	John Beckett
Miles Dodd	J. Pattison
George Rushton	M. Smith
John Ellwood	E. Dawson
Tim. Dobson	C. Gaddes
Jos. Rudd	William Harrison
Thomas Fawcett	Thomas Ellwood

Fourth Round.

Jos. Slack	George Rushton
Thomas Fawcett	Jos. Rudd
Tim. Dobson	James Johnson
John Ellwood	M. Dodd

Fifth Round.

John Ellwood	J. Fawcett
Tim. Dobson	Jos. Slack

Sixth Round.

Tim. Dobson	John Ellwood

Winners of the Prizes.

FIRST TIME OVER.

First prize,	.	.	.	.	Jos. Dobson
Second ditto	.	.	.	.	Jos. Stamper
Third ditto	.	.	.	.	Jos. Wills
Fourth ditto	.	.	.	.	W. Robinson

SECOND TIME OVER.

First prize,	.	.	.	.	Tim. Dobson
Second ditto	.	.	.	.	John Ellwood
Third ditto	.	.	.	.	Jos. Slack
Fourth ditto.	.	.	.	.	J. Fawcett

1830.

A meeting of the Subscribers to the Society was held at the " Admiral Duncan " Tavern, on Thursday, the 4th of February, and also on the following Thursday, to elect Stewards for the year. The following gentlemen were appointed :—

> Mr. Thomas Gordon
> „   William Richardson
> „   Timothy Dobson
> „   Edward Lancaster
> „   John Gaddes

Mr. Jackson Stainton was re-elected Treasurer.

The wrestling took place at Messrs. Hinton and Bayley's, the " Eyre Arms " Tavern, St. John's Wood, on Good-Friday, the 9th of April. Nearly 4,000 persons, among whom was a fair sprinkling of ladies, assembled to witness the sports. The weather was all that could be desired, and everything passed off in the most satisfactory manner. Over 200 competitors entered the lists, the sports concluding at half-past six o'clock.

After the wrestling a dinner was provided, at which Mr. Goulding presided, supported by Mr. William Richardson, as Vice-Chairman. The cloth having been removed, the Chairman presented the Prizes to the winners, as follows :—

PRIZES, FIRST TIME OVER.

First Prize, silver cup	. .	John Dixon
Second ditto, silver snuff-box	.	Timothy Dobson
Third ditto, ditto	. .	Thomas Thwaites
Fourth ditto, ditto	. .	Henry Mossop

PRIZES, SECOND TIME OVER.

First Prize, silver snuff-box	.	William Fawcett
Second ditto, ditto	.	John Atkinson
Third ditto, ditto	.	Thomas Bird
Fourth ditto, ditto	.	Joseph Stamper
Fifth ditto, gold seal	. .	John Ellwood

A silver pencil-case, for boys under 15 years of age, was won by Master John Beckwith.

A handsome gold key, for leaping, was won by Mr. James Johnson.

FIRST TIME OVER.

Fourth Round.

Stood.	Fell.
P. Thompson	B. Stables
H. Mossop	J. Pearson
C. Gaddes	Jos. Bullman
J. Dixon	Thomas Ellwood
Thomas Thwaites	Thomas Bird
Timothy Dobson	S. Fawcett
R. Hill	J. Gordon
J. Ellwood	M. Nicholson

Fifth Round.

J. Dixon	C. Gaddes
Timothy Dobson	R. Hill
H. Mossop	J. Ellwood
Thomas Thwaites	P. Thompson

Sixth Round.

Timothy Dobson	H. Mossop
John Dixon	Thomas Thwaites

Seventh Round.

Stood.	Fell.
John Dixon	Timothy Dobson

SECOND TIME OVER.

Fourth Round.

Stood	Fell.
Joseph Stamper	M. Potter
William Fawcett	Joseph Teasdale
John Atkinson	C. Holliday
Thomas Bird	James Atkinson
John Ellwood	Thomas Fawcett

Fifth Round.

John Atkinson	J. Ellwood
William Fawcett	Joseph Stamper

Thomas Bird, odd man

Sixth Round.

William Fawcett	Thomas Bird

J. Atkinson, odd man

Seventh Round.

William Fawcett	John Atkinson

1831.

The first meeting of the season was held at the "Admiral Duncan" Tavern, on the 3rd of February.

The following gentlemen were chosen to act as Stewards:—

Mr. Thomas Ellwood
„ Christopher Holliday
„ Philip Thompson
„ Henry Mossop
Treasurer, Mr. Jackson Stainton.

The sports took place at the "Eyre Arms," St. John's, Wood, on Good Friday, April 1st. Although the day was cold and uninviting, about 3,000 people assem-

bled to witness the wrestling, which gave unusual
satisfaction to all present.

Subjoined is a return of the wrestling, commencing
with the

Third Round.

Stood.	Fell.
John Carruthers	M. Potter
C. Gaddes	John Pattinson
Thomas Thwaites	William Wannop
A. Brown	R. Bailey
Henry Mossop	Joseph Wills
Thomas Ellwood	J. Capstick
W. Fenton	J. Slack
E. Ewin	J. Hewett
J. Teasdale	J. Cartmell
J. Stamper	Thomas Bird
Tim. Dobson	William Mitchell
S. Fawcett	J. Irving

Fourth Round.

S. Fawcett	G. Robinson
Thomas Thwaites	C. Gaddes
Thos. Ellwood	J. Carruthers
J. Stamper	A. Brown
E. Ewin	Tim. Dobson
W. Fenton	J. Teasdale

Fifth Round.

S. Fawcett	Henry Mossop
E. Ewin	Thomas Thwaites
Joseph Stamper	W. Fenton

Sixth Round.

J. Stamper	T. Ellwood
S. Fawcett	E. Ewin

Seventh Round.

Joseph Stamper	S. Fawcett

C

SECOND TIME OVER.

Third Round.

Stood	Fell.
H. Mossop	E. Hill
James Dixon	J. Lademan
T. Thwaites	C. Gaddes
J. Beckwith	J. Atkinson
T. Irving	P. Armstrong
P. Thompson	R. Sewell
J. Carruthers	Jos. Wills

Fourth Round.

H. Mossop	J. Beckwith
J. Dixon	M. Thomas
P. Thompson	T. Thwaites
John Carruthers	W. Wannop

Fifth Round.

T. Irving	H. Mossop
John Carruthers	J. Dixon
John Carruthers	P. Thompson

Sixth Round

J. Carruthers	T. Irving

WINNERS, FIRST TIME OVER.

First prize . . .	Jos. Stamper
Second ditto . . .	S. Fawcett
Third ditto . . .	Edward Ewin
Fourth ditto . . .	Thomas Ellwood

WINNERS, SECOND TIME OVER.

First prize . . .	John Carruthers
Second ditto . . .	T. Irving
Third ditto . . .	P. Thompson
Fourth ditto . . .	J. Dixon
Fifth ditto . . .	H. Mossop

The jumping was won by C. Holliday, clearing 17 yards 7 inches ; T. Railton was beaten by 7 inches.

Some of the most muscular and best proportioned men of the two counties were amongst the competitors. John Carruthers, J. Stamper, S. Fawcett, and Edward Ewin made some capital work. E. Ewin distinguished himself greatly by throwing Tim. Dobson, but was compelled to succumb to Fawcett in the sixth round.

---

1 8 3 2.

At the " Ship " Tavern, Little Bridge Street, Blackfriars, on Thursday, the 2nd day of February, a meeting was held by a numerous body of the subscribers to the Society, for the purpose of choosing the Stewards for the year. The following gentlemen were unanimously elected :—

> Mr. George Byers
> ,, John Pearson
> ,, John Dixon
> ,, Joseph Lightfoot
> ,, Thomas Thwaites
> Treasurer, Mr. Jackson Stainton

The wrestling, which took place on Good Friday, the 20th of April, at the " Eyre Arms," St. John's Wood, commenced at 2 o'clock, and was carried out with great spirit to a satisfactory conclusion. The following is a return, commencing with the

Fourth Round.

Stood.	Fell.
J. Lamb	R. Lamb
T. Ellwood	Campbell
C. Gaddes	R. Fawcett
H. Mossop	T. Abrahams

Stood.	Fell.
J. Gaddes	Jos. Dixon
C. Holliday	Gateside
Martindale	T. Robinson
P. Thompson	J. Carruthers

Fifth Round.

C. Gaddes	Thomas Thwaites
C. Holliday	P. Thompson
H. Mossop	Martindale
T. Ellwood	J. Gaddes

Sixth Round.

John Lamb	C. Holliday
C. Gaddes	T. Ellwood
John Lamb	H. Mossop

Seventh Round.

C. Gaddes	John Lamb

SECOND TIME OVER.
Third Round.

R. Margetson	Blackett
Thwaites	Campbell
Carruthers	Gateside
Abrahams	Bailey
Martindale	Fawcett
J. Wills	Taylor
E. Ewin	Coates
Thompson	Peters

Dawson, odd man

Fourth Round.

Carruthers	Dawson
R. Margetson	E. Ewin
T. Thwaites	T. Abrahams
J. Wills	Martindale

Fifth Round.

Carruthers	Thompson
J. Wills	R. Margetson

Sixth Round.

Stood.	Fell.
Carruthers	Thwaites
Wills	Carruthers

Jos. Wills, Champion

THE PRIZE FOR BOYS.

First Round.

James Pearson	James Lowden
E Fawcett	M. Johnson
J. Ewin	J. Bowring

Second Round.

E. Fawcett	James Pearson
J. Ewin	E. Fawcett

J. Ewin, Winner

Winners of the Prizes.

FIRST TIME OVER.

First prize	.	.	.	C. Gaddes
Second ditto	.	.	.	John Lamb
Third ditto	.	.	.	H. Mossop
Fourth ditto	.	.	.	Thos. Ellwood

SECOND TIME OVER.

First prize	.	.	.	J. Wills
Second ditto	.	.	.	J. Carruthers
Third ditto	.	.	.	T. Thwaites
Fourth ditto	.	.	.	R. Margetson

At the conclusion of the sports the Stewards adjourned to the dinner table. The chair was taken by Mr. W. Carrick, who, after the removal of the cloth, distributed the prizes to the successful competitors. The champion of the day, Mr. Gaddes, was much applauded for winning amongst so many scientific men.

1833.

The subscribers to the Society met at the " Ship " Tavern, Little Bridge Street, Blackfriars, on Thursday, the 1st day of February, and elected the following gentlemen as Stewards.

Mr. Joseph Stamper
  „ Christopher Gaddes
  „ Walter Graham
  „ Philip Thompson
  „ Richard Lamb
Treasurer, Mr. Jackson Stainton

At this meeting it was resolved, "That no person be allowed to propose or second more than one Steward, and that any person having proposed or seconded one, shall not be at liberty either to propose or second another; the proposer and seconder of each Steward to be answerable for his conduct, and debts due to the Society, and that the proposer and seconder shall pay, or see that the Steward, whom they have proposed and seconded pays every just debt, including the dinner tickets, due to the Society before the expiration of two months after the wrestling, otherwise all three shall be expelled the Cumberland and Westmoreland Wrestling Society."

The sports were held at the "Eyre Arms," on Good Friday, April 5th. The Stewards were Messrs. Wm. Graham, C. Gaddes, P. Thompson, J. Stamper, and R. Lamb.

Return of the wrestling from the

Third Round.

Stood.	Fell.
Jos. Robinson	James Atkinson
Jos. Teasdale	L. G. Dawson
J. Armstrong	John Beckwith
John Lamb	Thomas Abrahams
J. Carruthers	J. Richardson
John Thwaites	Thomas Beck
Thomas Thwaites	D. Dinglinson
C. Taylor	Thomas Irving
John Blackett	Thomas Gordon
Thomas Dixon	E. Ewin

Fourth Round.

Jos. Robinson	Thomas Teasdale
James Armstrong	John Blackett
Thomas Dixon	John Lamb
John Carruthers	John Thwaites
Jos. Thwaites	C. Taylor

Fifth Round.

Jos. Robinson	Thomas Thwaites
James Armstrong	Thomas Dixon
J. Carruthers, odd man	Jos. Robinson

Sixth Round.

J. Carruthers	James Armstrong

SECOND TIME OVER.

Third Round.

Stood.	Fell.
Thomas Abrahams	— Metcalf
J. Teasdale	C. Taylor
J. Brocklebank	R. Wilson
Jos. Wills	J. Richardson
D. Dinglinson	E. Ewin

Fourth Round.

Thomas Brocklebank	J. Blackett
T. Abrahams	Jos. Teasdale
Jos. Wills	D. Dinglinson

Fifth Round.

Stood.	Fell
Jos. Wills	J. Brocklebank
T. Abrahams, odd man	Jos. Wills

T. Abrahams, Winner

PRIZE FOR BOYS.

First Round.

Thomas Holliday	J. Pearson
R. Fawcett	M. Bird
J. Butterworth	J. Bowering
J. Parker	E. Fawcett

Second Round.

T. Holliday	R. Fawcett
J. Parker	J. Butterworth

Third Round.

T. Holliday	J. Parker

Winners of the Prizes.

FIRST TIME OVER.

First Prize	John Carruthers
Second ditto	James Armstrong
Third ditto	Jos. Robinson

SECOND TIME OVER.

First Prize	Thos. Abrahams
Second ditto	Jos. Wills
Third ditto	Thomas Brocklebank

BOYS.

First Prize	T. Holliday
Second ditto	J. Parker

1834.

The election of Stewards for the year 1834 took place at the "Ship" Tavern, Little Bridge Street, Blackfriars, on Thursday, the 31st day of January, when the following gentlemen were appointed :—

> Mr. Stephen Fawcett
> „ Joseph Peel
> „ Joseph Robinson
> „ John Compton
> „ Isaac Tomlinson
>
> Treasurer, Mr. Jackson Stainton

A resolution, that Mr. Philip Thompson's, "Peacock" Tavern, Maiden Lane, Covent Garden, should be the Society's place of meeting at the West-end, was adopted.

On the following Thursday Mr. Joseph Atkinson was elected a Steward, in the room of Mr. Isaac Tomlinson, resigned.

At a subsequent meeting, Mr. James Simpson proposed that the Society should offer prizes to two classes of wrestlers, viz. :—one for men of all weights, and one for men not exceeding 10½ stones; but it was considered that to deviate from what had been done in former years would be prejudicial to the interests of the Society.

The wrestling took place at Mr. Bowden's grounds,

" Chalk Farm " Tavern, on Good-Friday, the 28th of
March. The rain fell in torrents during the greater
part of the day, but, in spite of which, the sports
proceeded with great vigour. Towards evening the
weather assumed a more cheering aspect, at which
time nearly 3,000 spectators were assembled. After
the wrestling a large company sat down to dinner,
Mr. M. Potter in the chair. On the removal of the
cloth, the Chairman presented the Prizes to the
various winners, accompanied by a few appropriate
remarks to each. Mr. Robinson was loudly cheered
when called upon to receive the champion's cup. He
was a splendid wrestler, standing 6 feet 4 inches, and
one of the finest men in the Guards. " They were
giants in those days."

WINNERS OF THE FIRST CLASS OF PRIZES.

First prize, silver cup . . .	John Robinson
Second ditto, silver snuff box .	Joseph Wills Jun.
Third ditto, silver snuff box .	Stephen Fawcett
Fourth ditto, silver snuff box .	Nathan Robson

WINNERS OF THE SECOND CLASS OF PRIZES.

First prize, gilt silver snuff box .	Thomas Abrahams
Second ditto, silver snuff box .	George Brunskill
Third ditto, silver snuff box .	William Brunskill .
Fourth ditto, silver snuff box .	R. Wharton

The gold seal for Leaping was won by Thomas
Railton, Cockermouth. The prize for boys—a silver
pencil case—was won by Master Dawson.

COMPETITORS FOR THE SILVER CUP, &c.

Third Round.

Stood.	Fell.
Ed. Ewin	James Armstrong
Josiah Raisbeck	George Robinson
Joseph Wills, Sen.	John Cumpston
John Robinson	R. Carlton
Jos. Wills, Jun.	Thomas Abrams
N. Robson	R. Barton
William Dent	John Pearson
Thomas Bateman	R. Carruthers
S. Fawcett	R. Pearson
George Brunskill	Thomas Brocklebank
E. Dawson	E. Stainton
William Brunskill	A. Brown

Fourth Round.

N. Robson	George Brunskill
John Robinson	William Brunskill
E. Dawson	J. Richardson
Thomas Bateman	William Dent
Jos. Wills, Jun.	Jos. Wills, Sen.
J. Raisbeck	E. Ewin
S. Fawcett, odd man	J. Raisbeck

Fifth Round.

S. Fawcett	T. Bateman
J. Wills Jun.	E. Dawson
J. Robinson	N. Robson

Sixth Round.

J. Robinson	S. Fawcett

Seventh Round.

John Robinson	Jos. Wills, Jun.

COMPETITORS FOR THE SECOND CLASS OF PRIZES.

Third Round.

Thos. Thwaites	R. Bailey
William Dent	Thomas Irving
W. Brunskill .	E. Dawson
T. Bateman	T. Irving
T. Abrams	E. Ewin
G. Brunskill	J. Raisbeck

Fourth Round.

Stood.	Fell.
R. Wharton, odd man	William Dent
William Brunskill	Thomas Bateman
G. Brunskill	Thos. Thwaites

Fifth Round.

T. Abrams	R. Wharton
G. Brunskill	William Brunskill

Sixth Round.

Thomas Abrams	G. Brunskill

1835.

The election of Stewards for this year took place at the "Peacock" Tavern, Maiden Lane, Covent Garden, on the 5th day of February. The following gentlemen were chosen :—

STEWARDS.	PROPOSED.	SECONDED BY
Mr. N. Robson	Mr. James	Mr. Dixon
„ J. Richardson	„ Tomlinson	„ Robson
„ J. Peel	„ John Holmes	„ Compson
„ J. Pearson	„ Thomas Dixon	„ R. Lamb
„ Brocklebank	„ S. Fawcett	„ Stooks
SEC. & TREASURER.		
Mr. Jackson Stainton	Mr. R. Lamb	Mr. George Byers

At the same meeting, it was resolved :—

1st. That no person be allowed to propose more than one member, nor second more than another to become Treasurer, Secretary, or Steward. The proposer and seconder of each to become answerable for his conduct and debts due to the Society, and that the proposer and seconder pay or see that each

Steward whom they have proposed and seconded, pays to the Treasurer every debt due to the Society, including the dinner tickets, before the expiration of two months after Good Friday, otherwise all three shall have their names entered in red as having been expelled the Cumberland and Westmoreland Wrestling Society.

2nd. That a subscription be entered into for the purpose of purchasing sundry prizes the entire management of which to be left to the Stewards.

3rd. That each person subscribe 2s. 6d. or upwards and that none but subscribers natives of the counties of Cumberland and Westmoreland, who have resided in London, or within the Bills of Mortality, six months be allowed to wrestle.

4th. That there be two sets of prizes to contend for; one by men not exceeding 11 stones in weight and the other by the whole of the subscribers except the champions from this date.

5th. That a cup and other prizes the value of one third of the subscriptions be given to be wrestled for by men not exceeding 11 stones in weight. The winner of the cup to be ever after excluded from wrestling among the light weights.

6th. That no member shall, under any pretext whatever, be weighed for the light weight wrestling after two names have been called to contend for the light weight prizes.

7th. That the light weight wrestlers contend with the heavy weights for the remainder of the prizes, and the winner of the grand prize to be ever after excluded.

8th. That, after the above wrestling, no prizes shall be given for thrown men, as formerly.

9th. That a moderate prize be given to the best leaper at four hops and a leap.

10th. That in case of doubt concerning the eligibility of any wrestler who might (if eligible) win a prize, the Stewards withhold the same until they by his assistance prove the fact. Should he refuse this assistance, or not prove entitled to the prize, it be given to the next best wrestler, all minor prizes descending in the same manner.

11th. That the Stewards pay into the hands of the Treasurer, every Thursday night, all monies collected by them during the week, and that the names of the subscribers, with the amount of their respective subscriptions, be entered in a book kept for that purpose.

12th. That the Stewards select suitable ground for the wrestling, and make the place and the time of commencement known to the Society at least three weeks before Good Friday; and that they provide a dinner at some convenient tavern for the members to retire to after the wrestling.

13th. That the members request the Treasurer to

provide for himself and Stewards a suitable dinner after Good Friday, at the expense of the Society.

That the above rules be entered in the books of the Society and be, from this date, the only standing rules.

Particulars of the wrestling :—

11 STONE MEN.

Third Round.

Stood.	Fell.
E. Dawson	J. Woof
Thomas Irving	R. Cooper
I. Westgarth	C. Taylor
Thomas Hall	J. Campbell

Fourth Round.

I. Westgarth	Thomas Irving
Thomas Hall	E. Dawson

Final Fall.

I. Westgarth	Thomas Hall

ALL WEIGHTS.

Fourth Round.

Thomas Dixon	Thos. Bateman
George Brunskell	William Brunskell
T. Abrams	J. Robinson
Jos. Wills, sen.	Metcalf
William Wren	Charles Taylor
Jos. Wills, jun.	C. Gaddes

Fifth Round.

Jos. Wills, jun.	Thomas Abrams
George Brunskell	Thomas Dixon
Jos. Wills, sen.	William Wren

Sixth Round.

Jos. Wills, jun.	Jos. Wills, sen.

George Brunskell, odd man.

Final Fall.

Stood.	Fell.
George Brunskell	Jos. Wills, jun.

WINNERS OF THE PRIZES.

11 *Stone Men.*

First prize . . . . J. Westgarth
Second ditto . . . Thomas Hall
Third ditto . . . E. Dawson
Fourth ditto . . . Thomas Irving

ALL WEIGHTS.

First prize . . . . George Brunskell
Second ditto . . . Jos. Wills, jun.
Third ditto . . . Jos. Wills, sen.

The prize for leaping was won by Thomas Railton of Cockermouth.

1836.

Mr. Jackson Stainton presided at a meeting of the Cumberland and Westmoreland Wrestling Society, held at the "Ship" Tavern, Bridge Street, Blackfriars, on the 31st of January, 1836.

The principal business of the evening was the election of Stewards, which resulted as below :—

STEWARDS.	PROPOSED BY	SECONDED BY
Mr. John James	Mr. Peel	Mr. Snowdon
,, Jno. Snowdon	,, Pearson	,, Gordon
,, R. James	,, Holmes	,, Tomlinson
,, J. Harrison	,, Snowdon	,, Hayton
,, Westgarth	,, Graham	,, Dixon
SEC. & TREASURER.		
Mr. J. Stainton	Mr Holmes	Mr. John James

At a subsequent meeting, presided over by Mr. R. James, it was proposed by Mr. J. Holmes, and seconded by Mr. J. Snowdon, "That the sum of twenty guineas be paid out of the funds of the Society, *i.e.*, ten guineas to the Cumberland Benevolent Institution, and ten guineas to the Westmoreland Schools, as soon after Good-Friday as might be convenient to the Treasurer."

The following resolution was adopted at this meeting:—"That any member of this Society who shall publish, or cause to be published, a challenge to wrestle in the public papers, and any person accepting, or causing to be accepted, such challenge, shall be expelled the Society.

The wrestling took place on Good-Friday, the 1st of April, at "Chalk Farm." In consequence of the unfavourable state of the weather, the attendance was limited. Rain fell heavily during the morning, varied by snow and hail in the afternoon, which rendered the ground extremely slippery. The wrestlers, however, stuck to their work under these discouraging circumstances, although they did not much relish' their tumbles amongst the pools of muddy water which studded the ring. The following is the result:—

FIRST TIME OVER.
Fourth Round.

Stood.	Fell.
Joseph Wills, jun.	John Temple

D

Stood.	Fell.
T. Broklebank	N. Robson
John Harvey	E. Dawson
Jos. Wills, sen.	Jos. Dobson

John Rowe, odd man.

Fifth Round.

John Harvey	John Rowe
Jos. Wills, sen.	T. Broklebank

Jos. Wills, jun., odd man.

Sixth Round.

Jos. Wills, jun.	J. Harvey

Jos. Wells, sen., odd man.

Final Falls.

Jos. Wills, jun.	Jos. Wills, sen.
Jos. Wills, jun.	Jos. Wills, sen.

SECOND TIME OVER.

Third Round.

J. Harvey	Campbell
Robinson Ridley	J. Dixon
G. Blackett	Graham
T. Hall	Joseph Robinson

Fifth Round.

Robinson Ridley	G. Blackett
J. Harvey	T. Hall

Final Falls.

J. Harvey	Robinson Ridley
J. Harvey	Robinson Ridley

WINNERS.—FIRST TIME OVER.

First prize	. . .	Jos. Wills, jun.
Second ditto	. . .	Jos. Wills, sen.
Third ditto	. - .	John Harvey
Fourth prize	. . .	T. Broklebank
Fifth ditto	- - -	John Rowe

First prize . . .	John Harvey
Second ditto . . .	Robinson Ridley
Third ditto . . .	T. Hall
Fourth ditto · . . .	George Blackett

Despite the depressing effects of the weather, the sports were very interesting, from the fact that some of the best wrestlers of the day were amongst the competitors. The champion of the meeting, Joseph Wills, jun., exceeded all his previous performances, and threw his men right and left, as they came before him. Robinson Ridley, although not successful in gaining the first prize, made some splendid falls, and when he stood up with John Harvey for the final round, he was warmly received. The fine wrestling he had made during the afternoon, his well-built frame, and handsome appearance, rendered him a general favourite. However, although he stuck gamely to his man, he was compelled to succumb, after a well-contested struggle, and Harvey was declared the winner.

1837.

The election of Stewards, for this year, took place at a meeting of the subscribers, held at the "Ship" Tavern, Little Bridge Street, Blackfriars, on the 13th of January, Mr. Jackson Stainton in the chair.

The following gentlemen were chosen :—

STEWARDS.	PROPOSED BY.	SECONDED BY.
Mr. J. Peel	Mr. Halliburton	Mr. Stooks
„ G. Blackett	„ J. James	„ Westgarth
„ G. Byers	„ Stooks	„ Gordon
„ John Pearson	„ J. Peel	„ G. Lamb
„ C. Gaddes	„ R. James	„ T. Irwin
SEC. & TREASURER		
„ J. Stainton	„ Gordon	„ Pearson

The sports took place at " Chalk Farm," on Good
Friday, March 24th. The weather being fine, the
road leading to the " Farm," for a long time previous
to the commencement of the wrestling, was thronged
with people hurrying to the scene of action. The
bridge over the London and Birmingham Railway
was for some time blocked up with vehicles contain-
ing the more respectable portion of the spectators,
amongst whom were noticed many officers of the
Guards, who took a lively interest in the proceedings,
in consequence of some of the " Blues " and " Reds "
having entered their names as competitors. Between
6,000 and 7,000 people assembled round the spacious
ring. A great number of ladies were present, who
apparently took a lively interest in the sports. The
celebrated Primrose Hill, which rears its head on the
right, and every other eminence in the vicinity, bore
their full quantum of spectators, who had not the
needful to enable them to enter the enclosure.

The wrestling throughout was contested with the
most determined vigour, the soldiers seemed to be

pitted against the civilians, every fall was watched
with eager interest, and the spectators were under
one continued spell of excitement the whole afternoon. The most noticeable feature in the day's sport
was the *debut* of Richard Margetson, he had recently
arrived in London, fresh from numerous victories in
Westmoreland, and brimming full of chips and elas-
ticity. He threw his men well and gracefully, until he
was drawn against William Earl, of Cumwhinton, a
splendid wrestler, and much heavier than Margetson.
Earl was sometimes called the " great Earl," from his
strength and prowess as a wrestler. They were
loudly cheered on taking hold. The superiority of
Earl's weight, however, told in his favour, and after
one of the most exciting struggles ever witnessed, he
succeeded in buttocking his opponent very cleverly.
The result was a great disappointment to Mr. Margetson's friends on the ground, who were in hopes
that he would win the head prize. For the final falls
Corporal Wills, of the Guards(Red's), and R. Metcalf,
of the Guards (Blues), came together. The shades
of evening had been gradually closing over the scene,
and the contest could not be proceeded with, it was
therefore deferred till a future day.

There was a dinner provided by the proprietors of
the tavern, to which about 300 sat down. In the
course of the evening the prizes were awarded to the
successful men as follows :—

MEN UNDER 11 STONE.

First prize, a silver tankard . E. Dawson, Brampton
Second ditto, a silver snuff box R. James,   do.
Third ditto, a silver snuff box . J. Pearson, Longtown
Fourth ditto, a silver snuff box J. Butterwith, Kendal

ALL WEIGHTS.

First and second prize, cup ⎱ . Jos. Wills, senr., and R.
  and watch (undecided) ⎰ .   Metcalf
Third prize, a silver snuff box . J. Armstrong, Longtown
Fourth ditto, a silver snuff box . Thos. Abrams, Westmoreland
Fifth ditto, a silver snuff box . Wm. Earl, Cumwhinton
Sixth ditto, a silver snuff box . J. Wren, Penrith

Leaping—5 springs.

First prize—R. Margetson, beating J. Pearson and G. Blackett.

Thomas Railton was excluded, because he had
covered 17½ yards on a former occasion.

1838.

In consequence of the interference of the magis-
trates, the annual wrestling was held at "Chalk Farm,"
on Saturday, April 14th, instead of Good Friday.
A large number of spectators assembled to witness
the sports, which were managed in a very satisfactory
manner, some of the contests were very interesting,
R. Margetson distinguished himself by winning the
light-weight prize, throwing J. Armstrong easily by
the back heel.   In the final wrestle, between William
Earl and Thomas Abrams, an unfortunate dispute
occurred : on taking hold Earl slipped, but recovering
himself, threw his man and fell on him.   He was im-

mediately hailed the victor and carried round the ring, but the umpire ruled that in slipping he touched the ground, consequently Abrams was adjudged the winner. J. Allison, though unsuccessful, made some of the best falls ever witnessed. T. Hall was the favourite in the light weights, but, to the astonishment of every one, Murray, a youth, threw him by the cross-buttock in splendid style.

MEN UNDER 12 STONE.

Fourth Round.

Stood.	Fell.
R. Foster	J. Armstrong
R. Gill	W. Percival
H. Thompson	J. Watters

Fifth Round.

R. Gill	R. Foster

H. Thompson, odd man.

Final Falls.

H. Thompson	R. Gill
H. Thompson	R. Gill

ALL WEIGHTS.

Fourth Round.

Jos. Wills, jun.	E. Dawson
J. Wren	J. Robinson
William Earl	J. Wills, sen.

T. Abrams, odd man.

Fifth Round.

T. Abrams	J. Wills, jun.
William Earl	J. Wren

Final Falls.

T. Abrams	William Earl
T. Abrams	William Earl

The prizes were awarded as follows :—

ALL WEIGHTS.

First prize, 12 guineas . . .	T. Abrams, Westmoreland.
Second ditto, a silver watch .	William Earl, Cumwhinton.
Third ditto, a silver snuff box .	John Wren, Keswick.

MEN UNDER 12½ STONE.

First prize, a silver cup, 15 gs. .	H. Thompson, Shap
Second ditto, a silver watch, 8 gs.	R. Gill, Walton.
Third ditto, a silver watch, 8 gs.	R. Foster, Carlisle.
Fourth ditto, a silver snuff-box .	William Watters, Carlisle.

MEN UNDER 11 STONE.

First prize, a silver watch, 12 gs.	R. Margetson, Kirbystephen.
Second ditto, a silver watch 8 gs.	J. Armstrong, Longtown.
Third ditto, silver snuff box 5 gs.	R. Farriday, Westmoreland.
Fourth do. silver snuff box, 3 gs.	Thomas Hall, Brampton

The prize for leaping was won by Thomas Railton, five competitors, 16½ yards cleared, 5 springs.

1839.

The annual sports took place at "Highbury Barn," on Good-Friday, March 29th. The assemblage was very numerous, and the wrestling the best ever known.

ALL WEIGHTS.

Fifth Round.

Stood.	Fell.
J. Wills, jun.	J. Wren
J. Haig	T. Abrams

Final Falls.

J. Haig	J. Wills, jun.
J. Haig	J. Wills, jun.

Some very exciting wrestles took place for this prize. That between Wiliam Earl and Jos. Wills, jun., was a splendid struggle. The "Great Earl" stuck to his opponent well, but was thrown by the hipe, amidst loud applause. T. Abrams hiped Ed. Stainton cleverly. The greatest sensation was caused when J. Haig and J. Carruthers were drawn together. Carruthers was a fine wrestler, and considered by many the champion of the London ring. Haig was fresh from the country, where he was well known as one of the best wrestlers of the day. When his name was called out, it got wind that he was the celebrated Jemmy Haig, of Scuggerhouse. The excitement was, therefore, tremendous when the men got hold; but it was soon all over, for Haig threw his man with the greatest ease.

MEN UNDER 12½ STONE.

Fifth Round.

Stood.	Fell.
J. Carruthers	J. Dawson
R. Margetson	J. Dixon

Final Falls.

R. Margetson	J. Carruthers
R. Margetson	J. Carruthers

R. Margetson and Dixon had a dog-fall. On coming together a second time, Margetson threw his man a splendid hipe. Margetson and Carruthers had now to wrestle for the head prize. The first hold terminated in a dog-fall. Carruthers hiped his man in the second trial, but lost his hold, consequently, the decision of the umpire was in favour of Margetson. In the third bout Carruthers again tried the hipe, which Margetson cleverly stopped, throwing him a clean cross-buttock. Margetson was loudly cheered for the splendid struggle he had made against such discouraging odds, Carruthers being a couple of stones the heavier man.

MEN UNDER 11 STONE.

Fourth Round.

Stood.	Fell.
J. Armstrong	J. Sandford
W. Nicholson	W. Faulder

J. Gregson, odd man.

Fifth Round.

J. Gregson	W. Nicholson

J. Armstrong, odd man.

Final Falls.

J. Armstrong	J. Gregson
J. Armstrong	J. Gregson

At the conclusion of the sports about 200 sat down to dinner in the large assembly room of the tavern. Mr. Joseph Peel presided. After the removal of the cloth, the prizes were handed to the successful competitors as below:—

ALL WEIGHTS.

First prize, silver watch, 12 gs. . .	James Haig, Scuggerhouse
Second ditto, silver watch, 8 gs.. .	J. Wills, jun., Flatt
Third ditto, silver snuff box, 5 gs. .	T. Abrams, Westmrlnd.
Fourth ditto, silver snuff box, 4 gs.	J. Wren, Keswick

MEN UNDER 12½ STONE.

First prize, silver watch, 12 gs. . . . R. Margetson, Kirbystpn.
Second ditto, silver watch, 8 gs.. . . John Carruthers, Carlisle
Third ditto, silver snuff box, 5 gs. . . J. Dixon, Life Guards
Fourth ditto, silver snuff box, 4 gs. . J. Dawson, Life Guards

LIGHT WEIGHTS.

First prize, silver watch, 12 gs. . . . J. Armstrong, Longtown
Second ditto, silver watch, 8 gs.. . . J. Gregson, Corby
Third ditto, silver snuff box, 5 gs. . . W. Nicholson, Westmrld.
Fourth ditto, silver snuff box, 4 gs.. . W. Faulder, Cockermouth

Leaping.

First prize, silver snuff box . . . Wm. Nicholson
Beating four others.

1840.

The Stewards for this year were :—

Mr. R. Margetson
„ T. Railton
„ Peter Clemetson
„ J. Beck

The sports were again held at the " Barn," on
Good Friday, April 17th, and were witnessed by an
immense concourse of spectators. The handsome
prizes offered by the committee attracted nearly all
the best men of the two counties. The celebrated
Jas. Haig, of Scuggerhouse, was amongst the heavy
weights. His name seemed to be quite enough for a
good many of them, and it was not till the fifth round
that he appeared in the arena. The contest between
Plaskett and J. Robinson was the best of the day.

Plaskett was a light weight, and Robinson 6 feet 4
inches, (winner of the all weight prize in 1834), and
over 16 stones. Robinson lifted him up like a cat lifting
a mouse, when, Plaskett immediately put in the hank.
Robinson tried to throw him several times, but Plaskett
changed legs each time, and there they stood for some
minutes, the little-un, watching his opportunity, while
held up aloft in the arms of his powerful apponent, re-
leased him from the bank, made a sudden leap to the
ground, crossed the giant, both legs, and laid him
sprawling on the green sward before he could say
"Jack Robinson." It was a most exciting struggle,
and the victor was cheered over and over again. The
enthusiasm of the spectators was now thoroughly
awakened, and when G. Brunskill and Jas. Haig came
together for the final falls in the heavy weights, the excitement was at fever height. The men were a very
even match, as regards weight, but in height Brunskill
overtopped his opponent by 3 inches, his height being
6 feet 1 inch, while Haig stood about 5 feet 10 inches,
When they took hold, caution was the order of the
day. Haig, however, with his dangerous swinging
hipe, floored the soldier with ease, the next bout was
ditto repeated, and James Haig was declared the
winner amidst loud cheering.

The prizes were awarded as below :—

ALL WEIGHTS.

First prize, silver watch, 14 gs.   . James Hay, Scuggerhouse.
Second ditto, silver snuff box, 6 gs. G. Brunskill, Patterdale.
Third ditto, siver snuff box, 4 gs. W. Faulder, Cockermouth.
Fourth ditto, silver snuff box, 3 gs. T. Plaskett, Cockermouth.

MEN UNDER 12½ STONE.

First prize, silver watch, 12 gs. . . T. Abrams, Sowerby.
Second ditto, silver snuff box, 6 gs. . T. Donow, Penrith.
Third ditto, silver snuff box, 4 gs.. . J. Gregson, Corby.
Fourth ditto, silver snuff box, 3 gs. . E. Stainton, Troutbeck.

LIGHT WEIGHTS.

First prize, silver watch, 12 gs. . . T. Sandford, Crook
Second ditto, silver snuff box, 6 gs. . P. Clemitson, Stainton.
Third ditto, silver snuff box, 4 gs. . W. Brown, Carlisle.
Fourth ditto, silver snuff box, 3 gs. . R. Gill, Walton.

Leaping 5 springs.

First prize, silver snuff-box, 3 gs. . . George Lee, Longtown.

Distance cleared 18 yards. None of the other competitors had the slightest chance.

1841.

Mr. Robert Beck presided at a meeting of the members of the Cumberland and Westmoreland Wrestling Society, held at the "Old Drury" Tavern, Bridges Street, Covent Garden, on the 29th of Jan., 1841. The election of Stewards resulted as below:—

SECRETARIES.	PROPOSED BY	SECONDED BY
Mr. W. McCleave ⎫ „ John James ⎬	Mr. G. Lamb	Mr. P. Clemitson
STEWARDS.		
Mr. Clemitson	Mr. J. James	Mr. Lamb
„ Jos. W. P. Gill	„ Railton	„ R. Gill
„ J. Richardson	„ Stooks	„ Nicholson
„ Moat	„ McCleave	„ J. James
„ T. H. Halliburton	„ McCleave	„ F. Nichol
TREASURER.		
Mr. R. Beck	Mr. Halliburton	Mr. McCleave

The wrestling, which was of a very scientific character, took place at "Highbury Barn" Tavern on Good Friday, April 9th. The attendance was very

numerous, and the proceedings gave universal satisfaction. The entries included nearly all the best
wrestlers of the time. Mr. George Lamb, Cheapside,
supplied the prizes, which were handed to the successful competitors as below:—

MEN UNDER 11½ STONE.

First prize, silver watch, 12 gs. . J. Armstrong, Crosby, Cum-
[berland

Second ditto, silver watch, 10 gs. T. Plaskctt, Workington,
[Cumberland

Third ditto, silver snuff box, 7 gs. R. Margetson, Kirbystephen,
[Westmoreland

Fourth ditto, silver snuff box, 5s. J. Irwin, Bolton-gate, Cum-
[berland

Fifth prize, silver snuff box, 3 gs. J. Reed, Scotby Gill, Cum-
[berland

MEN OF ALL WEIGHTS.

First prize, silver watch, 12 gs. . G. Brunskill, Patterdale,
Westmoreland

Second ditto, silver snuff box, 10 gs. . E. Lamb, Swathburn,
[Westmoreland

Third ditto, silver snuff box, 6 gs. . R. Margetson, Kirbyste-
[phen, Westmoreland

Fourth ditto, silver snuff box, 4 gs. . J. Carruthers, Carlisle,
[Cumberland

Leaping.

First prize, silver snuff-box, 3 gs. . J. Dixon, Welton, Cum-
[berland

Details of the wrestling.

11½ STONE MEN.

Second Round.

Stood.	Fell.
G. Chambers	W. Watters
W. Brown	G. Brown

Stood.	Fell.
E. Lamb	P. Clemitson
T. Plaskett	Bertrand
J. Reed	R. Beck
Sandford	Lawson
J. Vaust	Hope
J. Armstrong	Donohoe
R. Margetson	James Boustead
J. Irving	E. Kendall

Third Round.

T. Plaskett	W. Brown
James Irwin	G. Chambers
J. Vaust	Sandford
R. Margetson	John Reed
J. Armstrong	E. Lamb

Fourth Round.

John Armstrong	James Irwin
T. Plaskett	R. Margetson

Final Falls.

J. Armstrong	T. Plaskett
J. Armstrong	T. Plaskett

At the end of the third round it was discovered that Vaust was not a native of either Cumberland or Westmoreland, consequently he was not allowed to wrestle any longer.

A fifth prize was offered to the five losing men in the third round.

The competition resulted thus :—

First Round.

Stood.	Fell.
John Reed	Sandford
G. Chambers	E. Lamb

W. Brown, odd man.

Second Round.

J. Reed	W. Brown

G. Chambers, odd man.

Third Round.

Stood.	Fell.
John Reed	G. Chambers
John Reed	G. Chambers

HEAVY WEIGHTS.
Third Round.

James Irwin	R. Fence
Thornboro	R. Lowden
Joseph Dixon	Sandford
J. Wills, sen.	E. Stainton
J. Carruthers	J. Dobinson
G. Brunskill	E. Kendal
E. Lamb	N. Farrer
R. Margetson	M. Morley

Fourth Round.

J. Carruthers	Thornboro
R. Margetson	Joseph Dixon
E. Lamb	James Irwin
G. Brunskill	J. Wills, sen.

Fifth Round.

E. Lamb	J. Carruthers
G. Brunskill	R. Margetson

Final Falls.

George Brunskill	E. Lamb
George Brunskill	E. Lamb

The prize for Leaping was won by Joseph Dixon beating four others.

1842.

The Members of the Society held their first meeting this year at the " Old Drury " Tavern, Bridges Street, Covent Garden, Mr. Richardson in the chair. The Stewards were elected as follows:—

SECRETARIES.	PROPOSED BY	SECONDED BY
Mr. John James	Mr. J. Holmes	Mr. D. Richardson
„ George Lamb		

STEWARDS.

Mr. Jno. Richardson	Mr. W. Fawcett	Mr. J. Holmes
„ Isaac Hopes	„ R. Beck	„ R. Gill
„ R. Brown	„ J. James	„ Geo. Lamb
„ R. Miles	„ R. Beck	„ M. Morley
„ A. Nelson	„ J. Richardson	„ Moorhouse

TREASURER

Mr. R. Beck	Mr. W. McCleave	Mr. Jno. James

The sports were held at the " Highbury Barn " Tavern on Good Friday, March 25th, and resulted as follows.

MEN UNDER 11 STONE.

First prize, a silver watch, 12 gs. . T. Hudson, Keswick, [Cumberland

Second do. a silver watch, 10 gs. . D. Harrison, Keswick, [Cumberland

Third do. a silver snuff box, 8 gs. : J. Swain, Cockermouth, [Cumberland

Fourth do. a silver snuff box, 6 gs. . R. Armstrong, Longtown [Cumberland

MEN OF ALL WEIGHTS.

First prize, a silver watch, 12 gs. . Jos. Wills, jun., Flatt, [Cumberland

Second do. a silver watch, 10 gs. . G. Brunskill, Patterdale, [Westmoreland

Third do. a silver snuff box, 8 gs. . J. Dixon, Welton, [Cumberland

Fourth do. a silver snuff box, 6 gs. . M. Morley, Keswick, [Cumberland

Leaping.

First prize, a silver snuff box, 3 gs. . Mark Morley, Keswick.

At this meeting it will be seen that Jos. Wills, jun., carried off the all weight prize, throwing Geo.

E

Brunskill and several other famous wrestlers. Mr. Wills, now Corpl. Major Wills, is at present (1869) Vice-chairman of the Society, and one of its oldest members, his connexion with the Association dating as far as forty years back.

The following is a return of the wrestling, commencing with

MEN UNDER 11 STONE.

Second Round.

Stood.	Fell.
R. Lowden	T. Huchinson
D. Harrison	J. Capstick
R. Armstrong	W. Stainton
J. Swain	Smallwood
R. Graham	G. Lancaster
T. Hudson	G. Armstrong
Bowstead (Guards)	J. Bowstead
J. Elliott	W. Thompson

Third Round.

D. Harrison	R. Graham
J. Hudson	Bowstead (Guards)
R. Armstrong	R. Lowden
J. Swain	J. Elliott

Fourth Round.

D. Harrison	R. Armstrong
T. Hudson	J. Swain

Final Falls.

T. Hudson	D. Harrison
T. Hudson	D. Harrison

HEAVY WEIGHTS.

Third Round.

G. Brunskill	G. Warwick
J. Wren	Bowstead (Guards)
E. Lamb	Miller
Jos. Wills, jun.	W. Carruthers

Stood.	Fell.
G. Chambers	Norval
M. Morley	J. Bowstead
J. Dixon	W. Stainton

Milburn, odd man.

Fourth Round.

G. Brunskill	Milburn
M. Morley	J. Wren
J. Dixon	E. Lamb
J. Wills, jun.	G. Chambers

Fifth Round.

G. Brunskill	M. Morley
J. Wells, jun.	J. Dixon

Final Falls.

J. Wills, jun.	George Brunskill
J. Wills, jun.	George Brunskill

Leaping—won by Mark Morley.

1843.

The following gentlemen were elected as Stewards for the Cumberland and Westmoreland Wrestling Society, at a meeting held at the "Angel and Crown," Wood Street. Mr. Robert Beck in the chair.

SECRETARIES	PROPOSED BY	SECONDED BY
Mr. George Lamb	Mr. McLeave	Mr. H. Moat.
„ John James		

STEWARDS.

Mr. Nelson
  „ Moorhouse
  „ Stooks
  „ Margetson
  „ Gregson
  „ Harrison

TREASURER: Mr. Robert Beck.

The sports took place at the "Highbury Barn" Tavern, on Good Friday, April 5th. The entries were not quite so numerous as on some previous occasions, but the wrestling was particularly good. The first prize for 11 stone men, was won by George Donaldson, of Patterdale, one of the best light weight wrestlers in England. In the heavy weights, Donaldson met his match in Jos. Wills, jun., who threw him cleverly. R. Margetson was very unfortunate, going down in the first round in both prizes. George Brunskill was again well up, taking the third prize for all weights. Mr. Moorhouse presided at the dinner and distributed the prizes to the various winners as follows :—

MEN UNDER 11 STONE.

First prize, a silver watch . G. Donaldson, Patterdale, Westd.
Second ditto, a siver watch, . F. Bowman, Carlisle, Cumberld.
Third ditto, a silver snuff box J. Bell, do. do.
Fourth ditto, a silver snuff box James Irving, do. do.

MEN OF ALL WEIGHTS.

First prize, a silver watch . Mark Morley, Keswick, Cumbld.
Second ditto, a silver watch . J. Norman, do. do.
Third ditto, a silver snuff box G. Brunskill, Patterdale, Westd.
Fourth ditto, a silver snuff box W. Smith, Cumberland

Leaping.

First prize, a silver box . . W. Rice, Westmoreland.

11 STONE MEN.

Result of the various falls from the

Second Round.

Stood.	Fell.
T. Dyer	D. Harrison
T. Thompson	G. Postlethwaite
J. Bell	T. Kirkbride
G. Chambers	J. Hetherington

Stood.	Fell.
J. Bowstead	W. Jackson
W. Philipson	John Scott
W. Smallwood	John Wright
James Irving	John Beck
F. Bowman	W. Mars
G. Donaldson	John Elliott

Third Round.

James Irving	G. Chambers
F. Bowman	T. Dyer
James Bowstead	W. Philipson
John Bell	W. Smallwood
G. Donaldson	Thomas Thompson

Fourth Round.

F. Bowman	Jas. Bowstead
John Bell	James Irving

George Donaldson, odd man

Fifth Round.

G. Donaldson	John Bell

F. Bowman, odd man.

Final Falls.

George Donaldson	F. Bowman
George Donaldson	F. Bowman

HEAVY WEIGHTS.

Third Round.

E. Gregson	J. Robinson (Blue's)
W. Smith	John Scott
W. Thompson	R. Nelson
M. Morley	D. Harrison
James Turner	J. Wren (Guards)
George Brunskill	T. Taylor
A. Nelson	Millburn (Guards)
J. Wills, jun.	Henry Mossop

Norman, odd man.

Fourth Round.

Norman	E. Gregson
W. Smith	W. Thompson
M. Morley	A. Nelson.
J. Wills, jun.	James Turner

Fifth Round.

Stood.	Fell.
George Brunskill	J. Wills, jun.
Norman	W. Smith

M. Morley, odd man

Sixth Round.

M. Morley	George Brunskill

Norman, odd man

Final Falls.

M. Morley	Norman
M. Morley	Norman

Leaping—won by W. Rice, beating four others.

1844.

The following gentlemen composed the Committee for this year :—

Mr. R. Margetson	Mr. R. Addison	Mr. A. Nelson
,, W. Fawcett	,, R. Farraday	G. Eilbeck
,, R. Beck		

Treasurer, Mr. M. Moorhouse.

The wrestling was held at "Highbury Barn," on Good-Friday, April 5th, when the prizes were awarded as follows :—

ALL WEIGHTS.

First prize, £8	.	.	. W. Millar
Second ditto, £4		.	. A. Nelson
Third ditto, £2	.	.	. R. Margetson
Fourth ditto, £1		.	. J. Haig

LIGHT WEIGHTS.

First prize, £8	.	.	. W. Morton
Second ditto, £4		.	. J. Simmons
Third ditto, £2	.	.	. J. Sill
Fourth ditto, £1		.	. J. Irving

Leaping.

First prize, £2 . . . J. Dixon

1845.

The Stewards for the year were:—

Mr. R. Margetson   Mr. W. Fawcett   Mr. A. Nelson
  ,, R. Beck   ,, G. Eilbeck

The sports took place at "Highbury Barn," on Good-Friday, March 21st. The prizes were awarded as below :—

ALL WEIGHTS.

First prize, £8 . . . G. Brunskill
Second prize, £4 . . Thomas Millar
Third prize, £2 . . E. Gregson
Fourth prize, £1 . . Mark Morley

LIGHT WEIGHTS.

First prize, £8 . . . Jeremiah Pearson
Second prize, £4 . . William Harrison
Third prize, £2 . . Thomas Earl
Fourth prize, £1 . . Joseph Pape

Leaping.

First prize, £2 . . . W. Mark
Second prize, 10s. . . Mark Morley

A handsome belt, with an appropriate inscription, was presented to the winner in each weight.

The sum of Ten Guineas was presented to each of the Charitable Institutions of Cumberland and Westmoreland.

1846.

The following gentlemen were unanimously appointed to conduct the business of the Society for this year.

CHAIRMAN.	VICE-CHAIRMAN.
Mr. W. Fawcett.	Mr. G. Eilbeck.
SECRETARY.	TREASURER.
Mr. R. Margetson	Mr. M. Moorhouse.

STEWARDS.

Mr. R. Beck
„ A. Nelson
„ J. Scott
„ J. James
„ J. Pearson
„ J. Nicholson ,
„ R. Lowden

The sports took place at "Highbury Barn," on Good-Friday, April 10th, and were very numerously attended. After all expenses were paid, the Committee presented the handsome sum of 40 Guineas, in equal proportions, to the two Benevolent Institutions of the two counties.

The prizes were awarded as below :—

ALL WEIGHTS.

First Prize, £8	. .	C. Dobson
Second ditto, £4	. .	Jos. Wills, jun.
Third ditto, £2	. .	James Haig
Fourth ditto, £1	. .	Jer. Pearson

LIGHT WEIGHTS.

First Prize, £8	. .	Jonathan Whitehead
Second ditto, £4	. .	Samuel Pearson
Third ditto, £2	. .	John Thompson
Fourth ditto, £1	. .	John Hawksdale

Leaping.

First Prize, £1 10s. . Joseph Dixon
Second ditto, 10s. . . William Duckworth

In addition to the above amount, a handsome belt, with a suitable inscription, was presented to the champion in each weight.

1847.

The following gentlemen were unanimously appointed to carry out the sports for this year :—

Mr. R. Margetson   Mr. M. Moorhouse   Mr. John James
 „ W. Fawcett   „ A. Nelson   „ G. Eilbeck

The wrestling took place on Good Friday, April 2nd, at "Highbury Barn" Tavern. The attendance was very large, although not quite so numerous as on the previous year, and the sports gave great satisfaction. The wrestling of Longmire, who was in fine fettle, was much admired, Robert Atkinson, the Sleagill giant, was thrown by A. Dawson, an amateur. The spectators were much delighted at Mr. Dawson's feat, and cheered him to the echo.

The prizes were awarded as below :—

ALL WEIGHTS.

First prize £8 and belt . . T. Longmire.
Second ditto, £4 . . . A. Dawson.
Third ditto, £2 . . . Joseph Halliwell.
Fourth ditto, £1 . . . R. Atkinson.

LIGHT WEIGHTS.

First prize, £8 and belt . . . Joseph Hallwell.
Second ditto, £4 . . . Jeremiah Pearson.
Third ditto, £2 . . . J. Chicken.

Leaping.

First prize £1 10s. . . . Joseph Dixon.
Second ditto, 10s. . . . Thomas Roper.

The sum of 20 guineas was handed to the two charitable institutions in equal proportions.

1848.

The Stewards for the year were elected as below :—

TREASURER: Mr. Moorhouse.

CHAIRMAN.	SECRETARY.
Mr. William Fawcett.	Mr. R. Margetson.

STEWARDS.

Mr. A. Nelson,
„ George Lamb
„ Joseph Wills
„ John James

It was resolved, this year, to discontinue the money prizes in favour of jewellery, cups, &c., and the following articles were selected for competition :—

FOR THE ALL WEIGHTS.

First prize . . . silver cup.
Second ditto . . silver snuff box.
Third ditto . . . silver snuff box.
Fourth ditto . . silver snuff box.

FOR THE LIGHT WEIGHTS.

First prize . . . gold watch.
Second ditto. . . silver snuff box.
Third ditto . . . silver snuff box.
Fourth ditto . . silver snuff box.

Prize for leaping . . silver snuff box.

The wrestling took place at "Highbury Barn," on Good Friday, April 21st. It was a splendid day, and a great number of spectators were attracted to the spot, among them a number of the officers of the first and second regiments of Life Guards. The meeting was a most note-worthy one, from the fact that the best men from the north had been induced to put in an appearance with the expectation of winning all the prizes, but in the heavy weights they were sadly disappointed, and the London residents remained masters of the field. The spectators were much delighted at the success of their metropolitan friends. Such a display of science, temper, and courage has seldom been surpassed and rarely equalled in athletic sports. The "man mountain" R. Atkinson, T. Longmire, Jonathan Whitehead, and Jos. Halliwell were all overthrown by amateurs.

ALL WEIGHTS.

Fourth Round.

Stood.	Fell.
J. Robinson	C. Dobson
J. Dixon	G. Wilson
J. Banks	J. Whitehead

R. Gash, odd man.

Fifth Round.

Stood.	Fell.
J. Robinson	R. Gash
J. Banks	J. Dixon

Final Falls.

J. Banks } Life Guards　J. Robinson } Foot Guards
J. Banks }　　　　　　J. Robinson }

To the surprise of all, Whitehead threw Longmire, and the giant, R. Atkinson, was thrown by C.
Dobson, Atkinson swung Dobson round four times,
intending to lay him quietly on his back, however, no
sooner had Dobson reached the ground when he made
a dexterous stroke at Atkinson on the outside, and
down went the giant. Never was such a scene of
excitement, handkerchiefs were waved, and hats were
thrown up in the air, the cheering lasting several
minutes.

MEN UNDER 11 STONE.
Fourth Round.

Stood.	Fell.
J. Halliwell	J. Dyson
R. Gash	T. Loy
J. Whitehead	M. Wills

Fifth Round.

J. Halliwell	R. Gash

J. Whitehead, odd man

Final Falls.

J. Whitehead	J. Halliwell
J. Whitehead	J. Halliwell

The final falls between Whitehead and Halliwell
were long and tiresome bouts, and wearied the spectators.

MEN UNDER 9 STONE.

Third Round.

Stood.	Fell.
T. Walker	S. Gill
W. Walker	J. Hunter

J. Rose, odd man

Fourth Round.

W. Walker	J. Rose

T. Walker, odd man

Final Falls.

W. Walker	T. Walker
W. Walker	T. Walker

Mr. W. Fawcett presided at the dinner after the conclusion of the sports, and distributed the prizes as follows :—

ALL WEIGHTS.

First prize, a silver tankard, 21 gs.   J. Banks, Life Guards
Second prize, a silver snuff box, 8 gs. J.Robinson,Foot Guards
Third prize, a silver snuff box, 5 gs.   Corp.Dixon,Life Guards
Fourth prize, a silver snuff box, 4 gs. R. Gash

MEN UNDER 11 STONE.

First prize, a gold watch, 15 gs. . . . J. Whitehead
Second prize, a silver snuff box, 8 gs. . J. Halliwell
Third prize, a silver snuff box, 5 gs. . . R. Gash
Fourth prize, a silver snuff box, 4 gs. . . Mark Wills

MEN UNDER 9 STONE.

First prize, silver snuff box, 5 gs. . . . Wm. Walker
Second prize, a gold pencil case . . . T. Walker

Leaping.—5 springs.

First prize, a silver snuff box, 3 gs. . . . R. Sherwin
17 yards 1 inch cleared

1849.

The members of the Society met at Mr. Clayton's "Sutton Arms," Caledonian-road, on March 20th, when the following officers were appointed :—

CHAIRMAN.	SECRETARY.
Mr. R. Thwaites	Mr. R. Margetson

TREASURER, Mr. M. Moorhouse

STEWARDS

Mr. J. James
" J. Stamper
" Rawling
" J. Pearson
" R. Margetson
" Wharton
" J. Chicken

The following revised rules were also unanimously adopted and ordered to be printed:—

1st.—That this Society shall be designated the CUMBERLAND AND WESTMORELAND WRESTLING SOCIETY.

2nd.—That the benefits conferred by this Society shall be confined to Natives of Cumberland and Westmoreland, to whom suitable Prizes shall be given to be Wrestled for on GOOD FRIDAY, in each year; the amount and number of such Prizes to be regulated by the Committee; and should any surplus money arise, that power shall be given to the Committee to decide the amount of Gift which shall be handed over to the Benevolent Institutions of Cumberland and Westmoreland; all such Gifts from this Society, be it understood, shall be equally divided betwixt the two.

3rd.—The Secretary shall read a Report of the Transactions of the Committee whenever the same shall be required.

4th.—Any Member of the Society having a Complaint to make, shall make it to the Secretary, in writing, who shall have power, at all times, to call a Private Meeting of the Committee for the dispatch of such business, and their decision upon it shall be final.

5th.—That the government of this Society shall be vested in a Committee of Seven Members, to be elected annually; and that the Committee shall have full power, and that all its transactions shall be binding until the election of the new Committee, at the Annual General Meeting; and that Four of the Committee shall be a Quorum.

6th.—That no person shall be eligible to be elected on the Committee, or become a Member of this Society, or be allowed to propose any Resolution, or Vote at any Meeting, who has not subscribed Two Shillings and Sixpence or upwards ; or be allowed to Wrestle, unless his Subscription has been duly paid up before the time of Wrestling.

7th.—That the Annual General Meeting of the

Society shall be convened by public advertisement, at least one Month before Good Friday, stating the Time and Place where the Meeting will be held, to elect Officers, and to receive the Annual Report of the Committee, which shall contain a general Statement of Accounts, duly audited; the Rules and Progress of the Society, and an accurate List of Subscribers.

8th.—That Five Stewards shall be elected annually to collect subscriptions ; and that out of the Stewards and the Committee, two Umpires and a Referee shall be chosen to decide the Falls in the Ring; and that the Stewards shall become Honorary Members of the Committee by virtue of their office.

9th.—Should any dispute arise in the Ring betwixt the Umpires, the decision of the Referee shall be final ; and any individual refusing to conform to the usual Rules of Wrestling, either by refusing to take fair hold—to wrestle over again, or otherwise— the Umpires shall have full power to strike out his or their names.

10th.—That should any Member or Members do any act to the dishonour or prejudice of the Society, either in the Ring or out of it, the Committee shall have full power to expel him or them from the Society ; but that it shall not be considered a disgrace for any Member of the Society to challenge another to wrestle, provided it is done privately, and not by public advertisement (with his knowledge and consent) ; but if any Member shall challenge, or cause another to be challenged by public advertisement, the Committee shall expel him from the Society.

11th.—That should any Member buy or sell, or offer to buy or sell, a Fall; or by neglecting to do his best, and thereby suffer himself to be unfairly thrown, shall be expelled from the Society; and any Prize that he may have been entitled to shall be forfeited by him, and given to the next in rotation.

12th.—That the number and amount of Prizes, and the different classes of Weights, shall be regulated by the Committee.

13th.—That all sums of money arising from Subscriptions, or otherwise, shall be paid into the hands of the Treasurer, every Thursday or other night when the Meetings take place, for the necessary expenses of the Society.

14th.—That proper Books shall be provided for the use of the Society, and all Receipts and Disbursements be entered therein, in such manner as the Committee shall direct.

15th.—That at the General Meetings of the Committee (at which subscribers shall be allowed to attend) the Treasurer shall produce his accounts of receipts and payments, and cash in hand, the particulars of which shall be entered as part of the Minutes.

16th.—That the Anniversary shall take place immediately after the Wrestling, when the Chairman shall deliver the Prizes to each successful Competitor.

17th.—That a Secretary be appointed, who shall attend the Meetings of the Society to take Minutes of the proceedings, and to produce the same at the sundry Meetings of the Society, to be confirmed; and that he be an Honorary Member of the Committee by virtue of his office.

18th.—That a Private Meeting of the Committee and Stewards be convened a fortnight after Good-Friday for the settlement of Accounts, and to prepare a proper Balance Sheet, to be laid before a General Meeting of the Society, which shall take place a fortnight after, when a dinner will be provided, at Two Shillings and Sixpence each Member. Tickets to be printed and circulated by the Stewards and Committee. That Four Tickets shall be allowed to each of the Stewards and Members of the Committee, at the expense of the Society; and that the Tickets shall express the Time and Place of Meeting·

19th.—That none of the Rules herein contained shall be rescinded, or altered, or new ones made, except at the Annual General Meeting of the Society; and that any Member or Members wishing to introduce any *new* Rules or Regulations, he or they must give notice of the same, in writing, to the Secretary,

at least one week previous to the Annual General
Meeting; and that none of the Rules or Alterations
shall be binding until confirmed at the General
Meeting of the Society.

20th.—That all the Rules and Regulations affecting
the Cumberland and Westmoreland Wrestling Society, heretofore existing, shall be null and void; and
that the present Rules and Regulations shall be the
governing Rules of the Society.

The wrestling took place at " Copenhagen House,"
on 'Good Friday, April 6th 1849. The handsome
prizes offered by the Committee again induced a
number of the professional wrestlers from the North
to take a trip to the metropolis. Foremost amongst
whom was the famous Sleagill giant, Robert Atkinson
taking the chief prize, Thomas Longmire of Troutbeck, " Bonny Longmire," the champion of England
for many years, Jonathan Whitehead, once the most
popular light weight in England, Jos. Harrington, and
Jos. Halliwell, all invincibles. That they should take
nearly all the prizes from their less experienced and
less muscular metropolitan opponents is not to be
wondered at. The committee, however, saw their
mistake, and the following year passed a resolution
that no wrestler would be allowed to compete who had
not been in London from the 1st of January of the

same year, thereby very properly confining the competion to residents in London. The Umpires were Messrs. R. Margetson, and J. James. Referce, Mr, Stamper.

Result of the Wrestling.

MEN NOT EXCEEDING 9 STONE.

Second Round.

Stood.	Fell.
J. Dixon	J. Robinson
T. Bradbury	T. Louis
J. Irving	M. Hodgson
T. Walker	G. Raws

Third Round.

J. Dixon	T. Bradbury
J. Irvine	T. Walker

Final Falls.

J. Dixon	J. Irvine
J. Dixon	J. Irvine

MEN NOT EXCEEDING 11 STONE.

Third Round.

J. Wilson	T. Matthews
T. Walker	R. Ellwood
J. Whitehead	J. Pattison
E. Cox	John Thompson

Joseph Halliwell and Jos. Harrington were an hour n the ring without getting hold, and were both blown out.

Fourth Round.

Stood.	Fell.
Jonathan Whitehead	E. Cox
James Wilson	Thomas Walker

Final Falls.

Jonathan Whitehead	James Wilson
Jonathan Whitehead	James Wilson

MEN OF ALL WEIGHTS.

Third Round.

William Miller	William Fawcett
Jonathan Whitehead	T. Hudsmith
Thomas Longmire	John Thompson
Jos. Harrington	James Brown
Robert Atkinson	John Dixon, sen.
A. Dawson	J. Pattison
George Wilson	John Dixon, jun.
Jos. Halliwell	John Thompson, Keswick

Fourth Round.

Thomas Longmire	George Wilson
R. Atkinson	Jos. Halliwell
Jos. Harrington	Jonathan Whitehead
A. Dawson	William Miller

Fifth Round.

Jos. Harrington	Thomas Longmire
R. Atkinson	Anthony Dawson

Final Falls.

R. Atkinson	Jos. Harrington
R. Atkinson	Jos. Harrington

The prizes were awarded as follows :—

MEN NOT EXCEEDING 9 STONE.

First prize, £5	. .	John Dixon, jun.
Second ditto, £3	. .	James Irvine
Third ditto, £1	. .	Thomas Walker
Fourth ditto, £1	. .	Thomas Bradbury

MEN NOT EXCEEDING 11 STONE.

First prize, £16 and belt . . . Jonathan Whitehead
Second ditto, £8 . . . . . J. Wilson
Third ditto, £2 10s. . . . . Thomas Walker
Fourth ditto, £2 10s. . . . . Ed. Cox
Fifth & Sixth prizes { Jos. Halliwell } Both blown out for
{ Jos. Harrington } refusing to take hold.
Seventh ditto, £1 10s. . . . . John Thompson
Eighth ditto, £1 10s. . . . . Isaac Pattison

MEN OF ALL WEIGHTS.

First prize, £24 and belt . Robert Atkinson
Second ditto, £10 . . Joseph Harrington
Third ditto, £4 . . Anthony Dawson
Fourth ditto, £4 . . Thomas Longmire
Fifth ditto, £2 . . William Miller
Sixth ditto, £2 . . Jonathan Whitehead
Seventh ditto, £2 . . Joseph Halliwell
Eighth ditto, £2 . . George Wilson

The total amount of the prizes awarded this year, including the three Belts, which cost £5, was £100.

1850.

The following officers were elected at the Annual General Meeting of the Society, held at the " Guildhall Shades," February 20th.

CHAIRMAN.   SECRETARY.
Mr. R. Thwaites   Mr. R. Margetson
TREASURER, Mr. M. Moorhouse

STEWARDS.

Mr. E. Stainton
„ J. Wilson
„ J. Pearson
„ J. Rawling
„ J. Dixon
„ J. Hartley
„ J. James

A resolution, proposed by Mr. Margetson, and seconded by Mr. Rawlings, to the effect that no man shall be eligible to wrestle in the London ring on Good Friday, unless he has resided in London since the 1st of January of the same year, was unanimously adopted.

The wrestling took place at Copenhagen grounds on Good Friday, March 29th. The day was cold, but, notwithstanding which, the ring was encircled by a dense crowd of spectators, to whom the sports appeared to give the utmost satisfaction. The army was well represented—Corporal Edgar, Corporal Dixon, and Corporal Robinson each winning a prize. Edward Stainton, whose name is familiar to all who have been in the habit of frequenting the London ring, was also amongst the successful competitors. George Brunskill again carried off the all-weight prize, and was loudly cheered.

Result of the wrestling :—

MEN NOT EXCEEDING 9 STONE.

First Round.

Stood.	Fell.
T. Wharton	Jos. Rudd
Gerard Raws	Thomas Smith
Thomas Langhorn	John Dodd
Rob. Yare	John Smith
C. Fawcett	Dockrell
Thomas Shepherd	John Andrews

Second Round.

C. Fawcett	T. Wharton
Gerard Raws	R. Yare
T. Shepherd	T. Langhorn

Third Round.

C. Fawcett	G. Raws

T. Shepherd, odd man.

Final Falls.

Thomas Shepherd	C. Fawcett
C. Fawcett	Thomas Shepherd
C. Fawcett	Thomas Shepherd

MEN NOT EXCEEDING 11 STONE.

Third Round.

J. White	R. Coulthard
P. Ward	J. Richardson
T. Bradbury	T. Langhorn
J. Dixon	J. Wilson
J. Monkhouse	G. Wilson
G. Kershaw	J. Harrison

T. Matthews, odd man.

Fourth Round.

T. Matthews	J. Monkhouse
J. Dixon	P. Ward
G. Kershaw	T. Bradbury

J. White, odd man.

Fifth Round.

Stood.	Fell.
T. Matthews	J. White
J. Dixon	G. Kershaw

Final Falls.

J. Dixon	T. Matthews
J. Dixon	T. Matthews

MEN OF ALL WEIGHTS.

Fourth Round.

Corpl. Robinson	J. Brown
Corpl. Edgar	E. Stainton
Corpl. Dixon	R. Lowden
Geo. Brunskill	W. Brunskill

J. Robinson, odd man.

Fifth Round.

J. Robinson	Corpl. Dixon
G. Brunskill	Corpl. Robinson

Corpl. Edgar, odd man.

Sixth Round.

Corpl. Edgar	J. Robinson

George Brunskill, odd man.

Final Falls.

G. Brunskill	Corpl. Edgar
G. Brunskill	Corpl. Edgar

Foot Race.

First, P. Sherwin, Cumberland
Second, W. Jenkins, do.

The prizes were awarded as follows:—

MEN NOT EXCEEDING 9 STONE.

First prize, £2 0 0 C. Fawcett, Kirby, Lonsdale,
Second ditto 1 10 0 T. Shepherd, Crosby, Ravensworth
Third ditto 0 15 0 Gerard Raws,   ditto
Fourth ditto 0 15 0 Thomas Langhorn, King's Meaburn

MEN NOT EXCEEDING 11 STONE.

First prize, £8 0 0 John Dixon, King's Meaburn
Second ditto   4 0 0 Thomas Matthews, Longtown
Third ditto   2 0 0 G. Kershaw, Hackthorpe
Third ditto   2 0 0 Jas. White, Eamont Bridge
Fourth ditto   1 0 0 T. Bradbury, Ravenstonaale
Fourth ditto   1 0 0 Page Ward, Carlisle
Fourth ditto   1 0 0 Jno. Monkhouse, Lorton
Fourth ditto   1 0 0 J. Harrison, Westmoreland

MEN OF ALL WEIGHTS.

First prize, £8 0 0 G. Brunskill, Patterdale
Second ditto, 4 0 0 Corpl. Edgar, Longtown
Third ditto, 2 0 0 J. Robinson, Wigton
Third ditto, 2 0 0 Corpl. Robinson, Warcup
Fourth ditto, 1 0 0 Corpl. Dixon, Cumberland
Fourth ditto, 1 0 0 W. Brunskill, Westmoreland
Fourth ditto, 1 0 0 R. Lowden, Broughsowerby
Fourth ditto, 1 0 0 Edward Stainton, Troutbeck

In addition to the above, the champion of each weight was presented with a handsome belt.

1851.

A meeting was convened by the Secretary at the "Guildhall Shades," on the 29th November, 1850, to decide about the removal of the wrestling to a more convenient place, at the grounds of Mr. Stones, at Hornsey Wood House, when it was resolved that the annual sports on Good Friday, 1851, should be held there.

The following officers were also appointed for the year :—

CHAIRMAN,
Mr. R. Thwaites.

SECRETARY,
Mr. R. Margetson,

TREASURER, Mr. M. Moorhouse.

STEWARDS.

Mr. T. Westmoreland
„   J. Richardson
„   H. Muckalt
„   Page Ward
„   J. Wilson
„   J. Dixon
„   J. Rawlings
„   J. James

It was resolved that all entries be made on or before the 16th of April, and any wrestler neglecting to enter his name and pay his subscription by that date, should not be allowed to wrestle on Good Friday. Five minutes to be allowed for the wrestlers to get hold; the names to be crossed out if the hold be not got by that time, at the discretion of the Umpires; and if either party refuses to stand chest to chest, with shoulders on a level with those of his opponent, and chin above, he shall be disqualified. Time allowed to slip hold, and after that the man that first puts down his head to be blown out.

The wrestling took place at Hornsey Wood House, on Good Friday, April 18th. The weather proved favourable, and an immense crowd of spectators assembled to witness the sports. The receipts were above the average of former years, and the assembly even more select than usual. Excellent accommodation was afforded by the marquee (erected by Mr. Stones), both to the wrestlers and the public; and as the programme consisted of only two classes of prizes, the sports concluded at an early hour. The most exciting wrestle of the day occurred in the second round of the heavy weight prize, when Edward Stainton threw George Brunskill, after this it might have been reasonably expected that Ned would come a long way towards winning, but the glorious uncertainty of the third round demolished his chance, as he was thrown at that stage by John Thompson. It will be seen that Matthew Palmer, of Peter's Crook, Bewcastle, gained a prize in the heavy weights. Matthew was never a clever wrestler, but his brothers, Walter Palmer and John Palmer, were thought the best men of their weight that Cumberland ever produced. In 1851, John Palmer carried off the heavy and light weight prizes at Carlisle, a feat unparalleled in wrestling history. He was heard to remark to a friend, on the first day of the wrestling, that he felt a superhuman strength within him, and did not believe mortal man could " fell " him. This proved to be the case, for he threw all that came before him, big and little; Walter was a much prettier wrestler than John. His hipe has never been equalled, and his outside chip was simply—perfection.

The Umpires were Mr. Jas. Wilson and Mr. Thos. Westmoreland; Referee, Mr. Richard Margetson.

Result of the wrestling :—

MEN UNDER 11 STONE.

Third Round.

Stood.	Fell.
Geo. Kershaw	Tho. Williamson
G. Irving	R. Nicholson
Jno. Steel	Wilford Stoker
John Dixon	Geo. Wilson

Jos. Scott, odd man.

Fourth Round.

John Steel	Jos. Scott
Geo. Irving	G. Kershaw
John Dixon	John Todd

Fifth Round.

G. Irving	J. Steel

John Dixon, odd man

Final Falls.

G. Irving	J. Dixon
J. Dixon	G. Irving
G. Irving	Dixon

The heavy weight prize was carried off by John Dixon, of King's Meaburn, a light weight wrestler. He won the light weight prize the previous year, and only lost it by one on this occasion, and he now gained the laurels in this unequal contest with some of the best men of the heavy division; Dixon was under 11 stone, and his success was rewarded with immense cheering. After the sports were ended a great number sat down to dinner. The Chairman, Mr. R. Thwaites, eulogized the orderly and straightforward conduct of the competitors, and trusted that the contests they had been engaged in would be an example to all to persevere in upholding the sport that to all and every one having a recollection of his boyhood's happy hours, was the medium of whiling away many a tedious leisure, and a stimulant to perseverance which he trusted they had benefitted from in later years.

ALL WEIGHTS.

Fourth Round.

Stood.	Fell.
Sergt. Chalmers	Thomas Marrs
Thomas Atkinson	John Thompson
Corpl. Dixon	M. Palmer
John Dixon	John Robinson
N. Cain	R. Richardson

Fifth Round.

Corpl. Dixon	T. Atkinson
John Dixon	N. Cain

Sergeant Chalmers, odd man.

Sixth Round.

Corpl. Dixon   Sergt. Chalmers
John Dixon, odd man.

Final Falls.

John Dixon   Corpl. Dixon
John Dixon   Corpl. Dixon

Foot Race.

First prize, £1 5s. .   .   Corporal Gregson
Second ditto, 10s. .   .   Peter Sherwin
Third ditto, 5s.   .   .   F. Williamson

The prizes were awarded as follows :—

LIGHT WEIGHTS.

First prize, £8 .   .   George Irving, Coldstream
                                 [Guards
Second ditto, £4   .   John Dixon, King's Meaburn
Third ditto, £2.   .   John Steel, Walby
Fourth ditto, £2 .   .   John Todd, Brampton
Fifth ditto, £1 .   .   George Kershaw, Hackthorp
Sixth ditto, £1 .   .   Jos. Scott, Keswick
Seventh ditto, £1   .   George Wilson, Greystock
Eighth ditto, £1   .   W. Stocker, Windermere

ALL WEIGHTS.

First prize, £8 .   .   John Dixon, King's Meaburn
Second ditto, £4   .   Corporal J. Dixon, Welton
Third ditto, £2   .   Sergeant Chalmers, Brampton
Fourth ditto, £2   .   Nelson Cain, Workington
Fifth ditto, £1 .   .   Thomas Atkinson, Old Town

Sixth prize, £1 .   .   R. Richardson, Warcop
Seventh ditto, £1   .   J. Robinson, Greystock
Eighth ditto, £1   .   Matthew Palmer, Bewcastle

A handsome belt was presented to the champion of each weight.

----

1 8 5 2 .

The following officers were appointed at the first general meeting of the Society, held at the " Guild-hall Shades," on the 25th of February.

CHAIRMAN.   SECRETARY.
Mr. J. James   Mr. R. Margetson

TREASURER, Mr. Moorhouse

STEWARDS.
Mr. G. Wharton
 „ J. Dixon
 „ J. Wills, senior
 „ J. Richardson
 „ J. Chicken
 „ J. Wilson
 „ J. Brown
 „ T. Westmoreland

The wrestling took place on Good Friday, April 9th, at Hornsey Wood House, and is thus described by Mr. Margetson in his report of the meeting:

" Good Friday was a brilliant day, and with gleeful hearts and blithe countenances, the natives of the North welcomed the cheering rays of the morning sun, as they thronged in hundreds to witness and participate in the sports endeared to them from their earliest years, many a heart panting with the eager hope of obtaining distinction in the wrestling ring which their far off friends might be proud to hear." It is the highest ambition of the majority of the natives of Cumberland and Westmoreland, when they arrive in the metropolis, to distinguigh themselves in the one grand pastime of the border; military renown gained by the soldier, or university honours by the student, carries with it no more pride than does the acquisition of laurels by the northern wrestlers in the London ring.

The entries were not very numerous, but the list included some good men, in the front rank of which stood John Dixon, King's Meaburn, who won the all-weights' prize, the third prize in the light weights also falling to his share. Alexander Scott, brother to the celebrated James Scott, of Carlisle, made his first appearance this year, and carried off the first prize for light-weight men, and the second prize for men of all weights. The Umpires were Messrs. J. Wilson and T. Westmoreland. Referee, Mr. Margetson.

Result of the Wrestling :—

MEN NOT EXCEEDING 11 STONE.

Third Round.

Stood.	Fell.
John Dixon	John Harrison
James Bishop	Geo. Irving
T. Williamson	Frank Moore
R. Longstaff	John Todd

A. Scott, odd man.

Fourth Round.

A. Scott	R. Longstaff
J. Bishop	T. Williamson

Fifth Round.

James Bishop	John Dixon

A. Scott, odd man

Final Falls.

James Bishop	A. Scott
A. Scott	James Bishop
A. Scott	James Bishop

MEN OF ALL WEIGHTS.

Third Round.

Thomas Whitfield	William Hadden
John Baxter	Thomas Atkinson
W. Stoker	Peter Crawley
James Johnson	R. Greenhow
John Dixon	John Wilkinson
A. Scott	Henry Murray
George Irving	James Martin

Corporal Dixon, odd man.

Fourth Round.

J. Dixon	Corporal Dixon
A. Scott	George Irving
James Johnson	W. Stoker
Thomas Whitfield	J. Baxter

Fifth Round.

Stood.	Fell.
A. Scott	James Johnson
John Dixon	Thomas Whitfield

Final Falls.

A. Scott	John Dixon
John Dixon	A. Scott
John Dixon	A. Scott

The Foot Race was won by Sergeant Chalmers.
The prizes were awarded as follows :—

LIGHT WEIGHTS.

First prize, £10 and Belt . Alexander Scott, Carlisle.
Second ditto, £5 . . . James Bishop, Bewcastle.
Third ditto, £3 10 . . John Dixon, King's Meaburn.
Fourth ditto, £3 10s . . T. Wilkinson, Lamonby.
Fifth ditto, £1 . . . R. Longstaff, Boroughsowerby.
Sixth ditto, £1 . . . J. Todd, Brampton.
Seventh ditto, £1 . . . Frank Moore, Nichol Forest.
Eighth ditto, £1 . . . G. Irving, Coldstream Guards.

ALL WEIGHTS.

First prize, £10 and Belt . John Dixon, King's Meaburn.
Second ditto, £5 . . A. Scott, Carlisle.
Third ditto, £3 10s. . . T. Whitfield, do.
Fourth ditto, £3 10s. . . J. Johnson, Temple Sowerby.
Fifth ditto, £1 . . John Baxter, Cumberland.
Sixth ditto, £1 . . W. Stoker, Windermere.
Seventh ditto, £1 . . G. Irving, Coldstream Guards
Eighth ditto, £1 . . Corporal Dixon, Life Guards.

1852.

A second meeting was held this year, and a prize of £10 was offered to be wrestled for on the 28th of June. It rained hard all day, and as the sports took place in the open ground, the attendance, both of wrestlers and spectators was very limited.

The following is a result of the day's wrestling :—

First prize, £4 . . . J Greenhow
Second ditto, £2 . . J. Hinde
Third ditto, £1 . . . T. Teasdale
Fourth ditto, £1 . . G. Irving, Coldstream
[Guards

EIGHT LAST STANDERS.

First prize, £1 . . . J. Moss
Second ditto, 10s. . . Alexander Scott
Third ditto, 5s. . . . T. Teasdale

1853.

The Annual General Meeting took place at the " Guildhall Shades," on the 9th of February. The Secretary read a report, showing the increasing prosperity of the Society.

The following officers were appointed to carry out the sports :—

CHAIRMAN.   SECRETARY.
Mr. J. James   R. Margetson
TREASURER, M. Moorhouse

STEWARDS.

Mr. T. Westmoreland
„ J. Brown
„ J. Chicken
„ G. Wharton
„ J. Rawlings
„ J. Richardson
„ E. Stainton
„ J. Dixon

At a meeting held at Mr. Wharton's, Windmill Street, a letter was read from Mr. James Irwin, an old subscriber, enquiring whether, in the event of his coming to London previous to Good Friday, he would be allowed to wrestle. It was decided by the committee that he should be allowed to compete for the prizes, as the rule excluding those who had not resided in London since the 1st of January, did not apply to old subscribers who had formerly a fixed residence in the metropolis, nor to the military, whose duties frequently caused their absence, but was intended solely to prevent men coming fresh from the North to take away the prizes.

The sports took place at Hornsey Wood House, on Good Friday, March 25th. The day most anxiously looked forward to by the natives of Cumberland and Westmoreland, was ushered in by a heavy fall of snow; this unfortunate circumstance, however, had no effect on the success of the meeting, the attendance of spectators being unusually large, and the wrestling, if anything, more interesting than ever.

The Umpires were Messrs. T. Westmoreland and J. Richardson. Referee, Mr. R. Margetson.

Result of the wrestling :—

Third Round.

Stood	Fell.
Matthew Palmer	Sergeant Chalmers
H. Howe	J. Little
T. Williamson	W. Douglas
E. Stanley	E. Sargeson

Fourth Round.

H. Howe	E. Stanley
T. Williamsom	Matthew Palmer

Final Falls.

T. Williamson	H. Howe
T. Williamson	H. Howe

MEN OF ALL WEIGHTS.

Third Round.

J. Hind	W. Robinson
H. Todd	Jos. Scott
Thomas Todd	Corporal Bowstead
G. Brunskill	Thomas Atkinson
H. Howe	Sergeant Chalmers

J. Tiffin, odd man

Fourth Round.

H. Howe	J. Tiffin
G. Brunskill	H. Todd
T. Todd	R. Greenhow

(blown out for putting down his head)

T. Hind, odd man

Fifth Round.

T. Todd	J. Hind
G. Brunskill	H. Howe

Final Falls.

G. Brunskill	Thomas Todd
Thomas Todd	G. Brunskill
Thomas Todd	G. Brunskill

Foot Race.

Sergeant Chalmers . .	First
P. Sherwin . . .	Second

The prizes were awarded as follows :—

LIGHT WEIGHTS.

First prize; £8 . .	Thomas Williamson, Sowerby
Second ditto, £4 .	Harry Howe, Abbey Holme
Third ditto, £2 . .	Matthew Palmer, Bewcastle
Fourth ditto, £2 .	E. Stanley, Workington
Fifth ditto, £1 . .	E. Sargeson, Brampton
Sixth ditto, £1 . .	Walter Douglas, Lorton
Seventh ditto, £1 .	J. Little, Aglionby
Eighth ditto, £1 .	Sergeant Chalmers, Longtown

HEAVY WEIGHTS.

First prize, £8 . .	Thomas Todd, Gilsland
Second ditto, £4 .	G. Brunskill, Patterdale
Third ditto, £2 .	Harry Howe, Abbey Holme
Fourth ditto, £2 .	J. Hind, Scotby
Fifth ditto, £1 .	R. Greenhow, Stainton
Sixth ditto, £1 .	H. Todd, Hayton
Seventh ditto, £1 .	Joseph Tiffin, Welton
Eighth ditto, £1 .	Sergeant Chalmers, Longtown

The champion of each prize was presented with a silver-mounted belt, appropriately inscribed.

1854.

The General Annual Meeting was held at the " Guildhall Shades," on the 27th January. After the Secretary's report had been read, the following officers were appointed for the ensuing year :—

CHAIRMAN. SECRETARY.
Mr. James Mr. Margetson
TREASURER, Mr. Moorhouse
STEWARDS.
Mr. Thompson
„ Westmoreland
„ J. Chicken
„ G. Wharton
„ J. Brown
„ E. Stainton
„ Bateman

An immense concourse of spectators assembled to witness the sports at Hornsey Wood House, on Good Friday, April 14th. The wrestling, especially for the light weight prize, was very good, and the performances were watched with eager interest. The celebrated James Scott of Carlisle was amongst the competitors; that prince of wrestlers carrying off the light weight prize in splendid style. About this time, it was remarked that there was a great falling off in heavy weight wrestlers, the light weights winning nearly everything. This is to be accounted for by the fact that wrestling was becoming a science in itself, and not merely an exhibition of strength, and that the heavy weights had failed to keep pace with their lighter opponents. Scott was then just in his prime, and stood a good chance of winning the all-weight prize; he was, however, compelled to succumb to Thomas Atkinson, of Old Town, Westmoreland, who threw the mighty champion of the light weights very cleverly. In the fifth round, Atkinson was thrown by Scott's brother Alexander, who won the second prize, George Brunskill, of Patterdale, gaining the first prize.

The Umpires were Messrs. Chicken and Westmoreland. Referee, Mr. Richard Margetson.

Result of the wrestling :—

Second Round.

Stood.	Fell.
Wm. Jackson	Alex. Scott
Andrew Mundell	Andrew Fox
Thomas Wood	John Bulman
Samuel Webster	Thomas Williamson
James Scott	Henry Ivison
William Smith	James Irving
Jos. Tiffin	Thomas Preston
Thomas Dickinson	Edward Wilson

Joseph Thompson, odd man

Third Round.

Joseph Thompson	Samuel Webster
Jos. Tiffin	William Smith
Thomas Dickinson	William Jackson
James Scott	Andrew Mundell

Thomas Wood, odd man

Fourth Round.

James Scott	Thomas Wood
Jos. Tiffin	Joseph Thompson

Thomas Dickinson, odd man

Fifth Round.

Jos. Tiffin	Thomas Dickinson

James Scott, odd man

Final Falls.

James Scott	Joseph Tiffin
James Scott	Joseph Tiffin

HEAVY WEIGHTS.
Third Round.

Stood.	Fell.
R. Greenhow	Thomas Dickinson
T. Atkinson	J. McGowan
James Scott	William Smith
George Brunskill	Joseph Tiffin
Joseph Thompson	Jos. Pearce

A. Scott, odd man

Fourth Round.

A. Scott	Joseph Thompson
T. Atkinson	James Scott
R. Greenhow	James Gibson
G. Brunskill	R. Rudham

Fifth Round.

A. Scott	T. Atkinson
G. Brunskill	R. Greenhow

Final Falls.

G. Brunskill	Alexander Scott
G. Brunskill	Alexander Scott

The Foot Race was won by James Scott, Carlisle,
The prizes were awardeed as follows :—

LIGHT WEIGHTS.

First prize, £8 . . .	James Scott, Carlisle
Second ditto, £4 . . .	Jos. Tiffin, Welton
Third ditto, £2 . . .	T. Dickinson, Brampton
Fourth ditto, £2 . . .	J. Thompson, Waverton
Fifth ditto, £1 . . .	Thomas Wood
Sixth ditto, £1 . . .	A. Mundell, Carlisle
Seventh ditto, £1 . .	Wm. Jackson
Eighth ditto, £1 . . .	Wm. Smith

HEAVY WEIGHTS.

First prize, £8 . . .	G. Brunskill, Patterdale
Second ditto, £4 . . .	Alexander Scott, Carlisle
Third ditto, £2 . . .	R. Greenhow, Stainton
Fourth ditto, £2 . . .	T. Atkinson, Old Town
Fifth ditto, £1 . . .	R. Rudham
Sixth ditto, £1 . . .	James Gibson, Musgrove
Seventh ditto, £1 . . .	James Scott, Carlisle
Eighth ditto, £1 . . .	J. Thompson, Waverton

A handsome silver-mounted belt, bearing an appropriate inscription was presented to the champion of each weight.

1855.

The Annual Dinner was held at the "Guildhall Shades," on the 23rd of June, 1854, when the following officers were appointed for the year.

CHAIRMAN.	TREASURER.
Mr. James	Mr. Moorhouse

SECRETARY, Mr. Margetson

STEWARDS.

Mr. G. Wharton
„ J. Brown
„ J. Chicken
„ T. Westmoreland
„ P. Milburn
„ J. Thompson
„ E. Stainton
„ W. Bateman
„ F. Bell

The sports took place at "Hornsey Wood House," on Whit Monday, May 27. The new Beer Act having come into operation this year, it was deemed advisable to postpone the Wrestling from Good Friday, to the above-named day. The weather was very unfavourable, and not a tenth of the number of spectators were present, who usually assembled on a Good Friday. The war in the Crimea operated most disastrously on the occasion, as at all the meetings hitherto, the stalwart forms of the Guards, and other fine regiments—abroad at the time—appeared conspicuous in the ring, and were wont to carry off many a well-contested prize. In addition to these drawbacks, Whit Monday not being a general holiday, is very unsuitable for holding a meeting of this kind. This instance affords a striking argument in favour of Good Friday. The umpires were Messrs. Chicken and Bell. Referee, Mr. Margetson.

A pigeon shooting sweepstakes took place this year, 10s. each with £5 added; 7 pigeons, 21 yards rise; charge of shot not to exceed 1½ oz.

R. Margetson (1st)	.	killed 6
J. C. Dixon (2nd)	.	,, 5
R. Fawcett	. .	,, 5
J. Just	. . .	,, 4
J. Hodgson	. .	,, 4

Messrs. Chicken and Sayer withdrew without shooting at all their birds. The tie for the second prize was shot off and won by J. C. Dixon.

Foot Race.

Eight started for the race, which was won by

S. Franklin	.	First
J. Duckworth	.	Second
R. G. Rudd	.	Third

The following is the result of the Wrestling

MEN NOT EXCEEDING 11 STONE.

Second Round.

Stood.	Fell.
E. Stanley	T. Winskill
A. Scott	Jos. Gaddes
Jos. Tiffin	Jos. Dobson
J. Moorhouse	J. Irving
B. Jenkins	T. Williamson
T. Wood	John Little

George Gibson, odd man

Third Round.

Jos. Tiffin	George Gibson
T. Wood	E. Stanley
A. Scott	B. Jenkins

J. Moorhouse, odd man

Fourth Round.

J. Moorhouse	T. Wood
A. Scott	Jos. Tiffin

Final Falls.

A. Scott	J. Moorhouse
A. Scott	J. Moorhouse

ALL WEIGHTS.

Third Round.

Stood.	Fell.
W. Shepherd	T. Swain
N. Faulkner	T. Atkinson
A. Scott	J. Nanson
H. Mossop	G. Gibson
G. Brunskill	R. Morton

Fourth Round.

Stood.   Fell.
W. Shepherd   G. Brunskill
N. Faulkner   Henry Mossop
A. Scott, odd man.

Fifth Round.

N. Faulkner   A. Scott
W. Shepherd, odd man.

Final Falls.

N. Faulkner   W. Shepherd
N. Faulkner   W. Shepherd

The prizes were awarded as follows:—

SHOOTING.

First prize, £5 . . . R. Margetson, Kirby Stephen
Second ditto, £2 10s. . J. C. Dixon, Bournes
Third ditto, £1 . . . R. Fawcett, Kirby Stephen

FOOT RACE.

First prize, £1 . . . S. Franklin, Kirby Stephen
Second ditto, 10s. . . J. Duckworth, Harkrigg
Third ditto, 5s. . . R. G. Rudd, Appleby

LIGHT-WEIGHT WRESTLING.

First prize, £5 . . A. Scott, Carlisle
Second ditto, £2 10s . J. Moorhouse, Hayton
Third ditto, £1 10s. . Jos. Tiffin, Welton
Fourth ditto, £1 10s. . J. Wood, Wigton
Fifth ditto, 15s. . . B. Jenkins, Milnethorpe
Sixth ditto, 15s. . . E. Stanley, Workington

HEAVY WEIGHTS.

First prize, £5 .	. .	N. Faulkner, Old Hutton
Second ditto, £2 10s.	.	W. Shepherd, Waverton
Third ditto, £1 10s. .	.	Alexander Scott, Carlisle
Fourth ditto, £1 10s.	.	Henry Mossop, Appleby
Fifth ditto, 15s.	. .	G. Brunskill, Patterdale
Sixth ditto, 15s.	. .	R. Morton, Carlisle

A handsome belt was also presented to the champion of each weight.

1856.

The annual dinner took place at the " Guildhall Shades " Tavern, on the 23rd of January. After the cloth was removed, the accounts were satisfactorily wound up, and the following gentlemen were elected to carry out the sports :—

CHAIRMAN. TREASURER.
Mr. James Mr. Moorhouse

SECRETARY.—Mr. Margetson.

STEWARDS.
Mr. Bell
 „ Brown
 „ Westmoreland
 „ Stainton
 „ Thompson
 „ Milburn
 „ Wannop
 „ Richardson
 „ Saul

It was arranged that the wrestling should take place at Hornsey Wood House on Good Friday, and duly announced in the public papers; but on the 9th of March, Mr. Stone, the proprietor of the grounds, received a notice from the police, forbidding him to allow the wrestling to be held on Good Friday at his place. It was therefore resolved that the authorities should be communicated with, and the following letter was despatched to Sir Richard Mayne, the Chief Commissioner of Police :—

"Islington, March 11th, 1856.

" Sir,—The natives of Cumberland and Westmoreland residing in London, have for the last century or more been in the habit of getting up a subscription among themselves for the purchase of prizes to be contended for in their favourite and national sports of wrestling, leaping, &c. ; and have (on account of this being the only general holiday in the year) been in the habit of holding their meetings on Good Friday—a day on which alone the members of the Society (being composed principally of young men holding situations in wholesale houses in the City) can be spared from their employment. These meetings were for several years held in the grounds of "Highbury Barn " Tavern ; but, on account of its greater convenience, have been held for the last five years at "Hornsey Wood" Tavern. From the highly-respectable class of young men comprising the Society—which is strictly confined to the natives of those two counties—no instance of the slightest disturbance or disagreemen has ever been known, a fact which the writer of this can vouch for, having been a member since 1826, and a competitor and winner of several head prizes. By way of precaution, and to satisfy the police authorities of the strictly respectable character of the Society, and the pacific and manly nature of its sports, the Committee have always been in the habit of engaging and paying for the attendance of a few policemen. Having, however, received an intimation from Mr. Stone, the proprietor of "Hornsey Wood House," that there is likely to be some objection made, on the present Good Friday, to the celebration of their usual annual sports, and being most desirous to avoid anything that may bear even the semblance of opposition to the constituted authorities, I am desired by the Committee to make this appeal to you, and to request that we may not be prevented meeting together as usual to enjoy our sports, so anxiously looked forward to and eagerly joined in at our annual gathering by nearly every Cumberland and Westmoreland man in London. To us this meeting is a festival; an assemblage of men from the same villages; of old school-fellows and friends who have known each other from childhood, and whose kindred tastes and early associations attract them to one spot, from the whole surface of this wide metropolis, to greet each other as such friends only can, and to view or join in sports which, from their earliest years, they have delighted in. As a proof of the respectability and high standing of this Society, I may point to the fact of the Earl of Lonsdale, the Hon. Colonel Lowther, Mr. Marshall, M.P., as well as several other noblemen and gentlemen being constant subscribers and frequent spectators, and that any surplus funds, arising from our meetings, have invariably been given to the charitable institutions of the two counties, as much as forty guineas having on several occasions been handed over at a time; I would also appeal to the police authorities in the neighbourhood, and state that the wrestling seldom commences before 3 o'clock, P.M., sometimes later, and that as the entrance to the grounds can be had quite unconnected with the house, it is not proposed in any way to interfere with the law of closing public houses; that no member belonging to the Society has the slightest pecuniary interest in it, directly or indirectly, but that every shilling which is collected is accounted for and spent in prizes, for the use of the grounds, or given to the charities as before-mentioned.

In apologising for troubling you at this length (which I should not have done if I could have given the necessary information in a smaller space), I beg to say that we will hold ourselves responsible that no breach of the peace shall occur, and that we will most willingly pay the expense of police on the grounds. Most anxiously hoping that you will not put your veto on the harmless amusement we have so long enjoyed, there being no other day in the year (as frequent trials have proved) on which we could possibly hold the meeting, your favourable and early reply will greatly oblige,

Sir, yours most respectfully,

RICHARD MARGETSON,

For the Cumberland and Westmorland
Wrestling Society.

To SIR RICHARD MAYNE,

Chief Commissioner of Police,
Scotland Yard.

Sir Richard Mayne's reply was, that the wrestling should be allowed to take place without interruption on Good Friday, and in addition to which the Society was to be supplied with as many men from the police as might be desired for the purpose of keeping order. The annual meetings of the Society were thus placed on a firmer basis than ever they had been since its first existence.

The wrestling took place at "Hornsey Wood House," Tavern, on Good Friday, March 21st. When it became known that Sir Richard Mayne had sanctioned the meeting on that day, the sports were looked forward to with the greatest interest, consequently, an unusual number of spectators assembled on the grounds. The wrestling was very good and gave great satisfacton. The only hitch in the proceedings occurred in the final fall between John Smith and Geo. Brunskill; Smith's knee touched the ground, but recovering himself quickly, he continued the struggle, and finally threw Brunskill. It was thought by those who did not see Smith's position, and others who did not understand the laws of wrestling, that he was the victor. The Umpires, however, very properly awarded the first prize to Brunskill. In the first round, all weights, Joseph Gilchrist distinguished himself by throwing Alex. Scott very cleverly. In the third round, however, George Brunskill finished his career by throwing him after a good tussle.

The Umpires were Messrs. Richardson and Bell, Referee, Mr. Margetson.

Result of the wrestling:—

LIGHT WEIGHTS, 11 STONE MEN.

Second Round.

Stood.	Fell.
T. Williamson	Watty Fisher
Alex. Scott	Wm. Leggett
R. Atkinson, jun.	Jno. Bulman
J. Moorhouse	Jno. Cooke
H. Howe,	Thomas Boustead
Jno. Thompson	Thomas Wood
Jos. Tiffin	Geo. Brown
John Little	Geo. Gibson

Third Round.

Stood.	Fell.
H. Howe	A. Scott
Jno. Thompson	R. Atkinson, jun.
J. Moorhouse ·	T. Williamson
Jos. Tiffin	Jno. Little

Fourth Round.

Stood.	Fell.
Jos. Tiffin	Jno. Thompson
H. Howe	J. Moorhouse

Final Falls.

Jos. Tiffin	H. Howe
Jos. Tiffin	H. Howe

HEAVY WEIGHTS.

Third Round.

George Brunskill	Jos. Gilchrist
Henry Howe	J. Foster
John Robinson	Jos. Tiffin
John Smith	Thomas Atkinson
John Haddecot	J. Morton
Thomas Wood	C. Nanson

John Thompson, odd man

Fourth Round.

John Thompson	Henry Howe
Thomas Wood	J. Robinson
G. Brunskill	J. Hadicott

John Smith, odd man

Fifth Round.

John Smith	John Thompson
George Brunskill	Thos. Wood

FINAL FALLS.

George Brunskill	John Smith
John Smith	G. Brunskill
George Brunskill	John Smith

The prizes were awarded as follows :—

Foot Race.

First prize, silver snuff box, Samuel Frankland, Kirbystephen.

LIGHT WEIGHT WRESTLING.

First prize, silver watch . . . Joseph Tiffin, Welton
Second ditto, silver snuff box . . Henry Howe, Penrith
Third ditto, silver snuff box . . J. Moorhouse, Hayton
Fourth ditto, silver snuff box . . J. Thompson, Skelton

ALL WEIGHTS.

First prize, silver watch, . . . G. Brunskill, Patterdale
Second ditto, silver snuff box . . John Smith, Old Hutton
Third ditto, silver snuff box . . Thomas Wood, Blencogo
Fourth ditto, silver snuff box . . J. Thompson, Skelton

The increasing state of the funds enabled the committee, this year, to present 20 guineas to the benevolent institutions of the two counties, 10 guineas were handed to the Cumberland Benevolent Institution in the name of Mr. Brown, and 10 guineas to the Westmoreland Schools in the name of Mr. Stainton. The annual settling dinner took place at the " Guildhall Shades," on the 18th of April, when the officers were elected for the ensuing year. Messrs. James, Margetson, and Moorhouse having declined to accept the offices of President, Secretary, and Treasurer which they had so long held, the following gentlemen were afterwards appointed for

1857.

CHAIRMAN.   SECRETARY.
Mr. W. Thompson   T. Westmoreland
TREASURER.
J. Stooks.

STEWARDS.

Mr. L. D. Lund
 „ James Brown
 „ James Hodgson
 „ T. Charlton
 „ W. Leggett
 „ J. Tiffin
 „ E. Stainton
 „ T. Williamson

The sports took place, for the first time, in the grounds of the "White Lion," Hackney Wick, on Good Friday, April 10th. The wrestling was of a very superior description, and reflected the greatest credit on all concerned; and, after all expenses had been paid, the sum of 20 guineas was handed to the benevolent institutions connected with the two counties.

The following is the result :—

LIGHT WEIGHTS—11 STONE MEN.

Third Round.

Stood.	Fell.
William Banks	T. Mein ·
James Bowman	E. Stanley
John Lancaster	P. Barnes
Jos. Thompson	Alex. Scott
John Smith	James Brown
John Thompson	E. Charlton
George Gibson	John Little

Fourth Round.

William Banks	J. Bowman
John Thompson	John Smith
Jos. Thompson	George Gibson

John Lancaster, odd man

Fifth Round.

Stood.	Fell.
Jos. Thompson	John Thompson

William Banks, odd man

Final Falls.

Jos. Thompson	William Banks
Jos. Thompson	William Banks

HEAVY WEIGHTS.

Third Round.

John Scott	John Wheatley
J. Thompson	James Brown
J. Ruddham	William Jenkinson
W. Banks	T. Atkinson
John Smith	George Brunskill

J. Nanson, odd man

Fourth Round.

John Smith	John Nanson
John Scott	William Banks
J. Routledge	J. Ruddham

J. Thompson, odd man

Fifth Round.

Jos. Thompson	John Scott
John Smith	J. Routledge

Final Falls.

John Smith	Jos. Thompson
John Smith	Jos. Thompson

The prizes were awarded as follows :—

LIGHT WEIGHTS.

First prize, silver watch	.	.	.	Jos. Thompson
Second ditto, silver snuff box	.	.		William Banks
Third ditto, silver snuff box	.	.		John Thompson
Fourth ditto, silver snuff box	.	.		John Lancaster

ALL WEIGHTS.

First prize, silver watch .	. .	John Smith
Second ditto, silver snuff box .	.	Jos. Thompson
Third ditto, silver snuff box	. .	J. Routledge
Fourth ditto, silver snuff box .	.	John Scott

1858.

The following gentlemen were elected as officers for this year.

CHAIRMAN, Mr. W. Thompson.   TREASURER, Mr. James Stooks.
SECRETARY, Mr. T. Westmoreland.

STEWARDS.

Mr. Lund
„ Gibson
„ Leggett
„ Gilchrist
„ Bulman
„ Charlton
„ Hodgson
„ Ellison
„ John Thompson

The wrestling took place on Good Friday, April 4th, at the " White Lion," Hackney Wick, and was well attended, although the weather was cold, with occasional falls of snow.

Mr. R. Margetson was Referee.

ALL WEIGHTS.
Fourth Round.

Stood.	Fell.
E. Calver	J. Smith
J. Wilkinson	G. Mason
T. Hetherington	R. Atkinson
Jos. Thompson	Jos. Scott

Fifth Round.

Stood.	Fell.
J. Wilkinson	E. Calver
T. Hetherington	Jos. Thompson

Final Falls.

T. Hetherington	J. Wilkinson
T. Hetherington	J. Wilkinson

LIGHT WEIGHTS—11 STONE MEN.
Fourth Round.

Geo. Gibson	R. Atkinson
J. Smith	J. Tiffin
J. Kirkbridge	J. Sanders

Fifth Round.

J. Smith	J. Kirkbridge

Geo. Gibson, odd man

Final Falls.

Geo. Gibson	John Smith
Geo. Gibson	John Smith

The prizes were awarded as follows :—

LIGHT WEIGHTS.

First prize, silver watch . .	George Gibson
Second ditto, silver snuff box. .	John Smith
Third ditto, silver snuff box . .	Thomas Sanders
Fourth ditto, silver snuff box .	J. Kirkbridge

HEAVY WEIGHTS.

First prize, silver watch . .	T. Hetherington
Second ditto, silver snuff box .	Jos. Wilkinson
Third ditto, silver snuff box. .	Jos. Thompson
Fourth ditto, silver snuff box .	E. Calver

A donation of twenty guineas was handed to the two charitable institutions of Cumberland and Westmoreland, in equal proportions.

1 8 5 9.

At the aniversary dinner held at the "Guildhall Shades" the previous year, the following officers were appointed to carry out the sports :—

CHAIRMAN.
Mr. William Thompson

TREASURER.
Mr. James Stooks

SECRETARY.
Mr. Thomas Westmorcland

STEWARDS.
Mr. L. D. Lund
  ,, William Leggatt
  ,, John Thompson
  ,, Thomas Hetherington
  ,, Thomas Mein
  ,, James Ellison
  ,, George Gibson
  ,, Jos. Gilchrist

The wrestling took place at the "White Lion," Hackney Wick, on Good Friday, April 22nd. This was a very successful year. In addition to the sports being the best that ever had been witnessed, the list of competitors included some of the best light weight men we have had from the north—viz., George Sanderson, G. Mason, J. Mason, Jno. Smith, J. Tiffin, &c. Mr. Sanderson's wrestling was much admired, and this being his first year in London, he received a hearty reception. It will be seen that he succeeded in gaining the second prize in the heavy weights and the third in the light. In his wrestle with G. Mason in the fifth round, light weights, it was the general opinion of those present that Mason was thrown, although the umpires ruled otherwise. They were drawn together again in the third round, heavy weights; on going out to his man, Sanderson held up his hand to the assembled multitude, and said,—"See if I don't 'fell' him this time!" No sooner had they got into holds, when amidst the cheers of the spectators, Sanderson hiped him in the most brilliant manner possible.

The following is the result of the wrestling:—

LIGHT WEIGHTS, 11 STONE MEN.
Third Round.

Stood.	Fell.
T. Robinson	J. Atkinson
G. Sanderson	G. Kirkpatrick
G. Mason	Jos. Thompson
J. Tiffin	J. Smith (lost hold)
J. Mason	J. Scott

Fourth Round.

J. Mason	J Tiffin
G. Sanderson	T. Robinson
G. Mason, odd man	

Fifth Round.

G. Mason	G. Sanderson
J. Mason, odd man	

Final Falls.

J. Mason	G. Mason
G. Mason	J. Mason
G. Mason	J. Mason

HEAVY WEIGHTS.

Third Round.

Stood.	Fell.
H. Tyson	G. Newby
W. Sewell	R. Atkinson
J. Mason	M. Robinson
G. Sanderson	G. Mason
J. Wills	W. Jackson
J. Wilkinson	J. Thompson
Thos. Hetherington	John Smith

Fourth Round.

T. Hetherington	J. Wilkinson
G. Sanderson	J. Wills
W. Sewell	J. Mason

H. Tyson, odd man

Fifth Round.

G. Sanderson	H. Tyson
T. Hetherington	W. Sewell

Final Falls.

T. Hetherington	G. Sanderson
T. Hetherington	G. Sanderson

The prizes were awarded as follows :—

LIGHT WEIGHTS.

First Prize, a silver watch .	. G. Mason
Second ditto, a silver snuff box	. J. Mason
Third ditto, a silver snuff box	. Geo. Sanderson
Fourth ditto, a silver snuff box	. T. Robinson

HEAVY WEIGHTS.

First Prize, a silver watch .	. Thos. Hetherington
Second ditto, a silver snuff box	. G. Sanderson
Third ditto, a silver snuff box	. W. Sewell
Fourth ditto, a silver snuff box	. H. Tyson

The sum of 40 guineas was presented to the two

benevolent institutions, in the names of the following gentlemen :—Messrs. James Hodgson and James Elli-son, for Cumberland; and Messrs. John Thompson and George Gibson, for Westmoreland.

1860.

The Annual General Meeting of the Society was held at the " Guildhall Shades," on the 7th of March. The principal business to be transacted was the election of officers, which produced some very smart competitions, especially that for the position of Chairman. After a very animated discussion, the following gentlemen were proposed, seconded, and declared duly elected :—

CHAIRMAN.	HON. SECRETARY.
Mr. William Thompson	Mr. R. Margetson

TREASURER, Mr. James Hodgson

STEWARDS.

Mr. John Thompson
  „   William Armstrong
  „   L. D. Lund
  „   Geo. Gibson
  „   Jas. Ellison
  „   — Wannop
  „   James Brown
  „   F. Bell
  „   T. Clemetson
  „   J. Richardson

The wrestling took place at " Hornsey Wood

House," on Good Friday, April 6th. The attendance of spectators was very numerous, all parts of the grounds being crowded. It will be seen that the heavy weights showed, as of late years, great inferiority, three of the prizes in that class were won by light-weight men, John Smith, the winner of the heavy-weight prize being under 11 stones, and always able to wrestle in that class. The Umpires were Messrs. Frank Bell, and John Richardson; Referee, Mr. R. Margetson.

The following is the result:—

LIGHT WEIGHTS—11 STONE MEN.

Second Round.

Stood.	Fell.
M. Robinson	John Illingworth
G. Mason	E. Oliphant
William Banks	Jos. Gilchrist
T. Robinson	T. Brunskill
J. Mason	C. Airey
William Atkinson	T. Smith
G. Sanderson	John Magnay
J. Kirkpatrick	W. Walker

Third Round.

G. Sanderson	William Banks
G. Mason	J. Kirkpatrick
M. Robinson	T. Robinson
John Mason	W. Atkinson

Fourth Round.

G. Mason	G. Sanderson
John Mason	M. Robinson

Final Falls.

Stood.	Fell.
G. Mason	John Mason
John Mason	Geo. Mason
John Mason	Geo. Mason

HEAVY WEIGHTS.
Third Round.

J. Logan	J. McGowan
T. Robinson	R. Atkinson
J. Hewitson	G. Sanderson
John Smith	John Mason
M. Robinson	T. Smith
W. Banks	T. Brunskill

Fourth Round.

T. Robinson	W. Banks
M. Robinson	J. Hewitson
Jno. Smith	J. Logan

Fifth Round.

John Smith	Mat. Robinson

Thos. Robinson, odd man.

Final Falls.

John Smith	T. Robinson
John Smith	T. Robinson

The prizes were awarded as below :—

Foot Race.

First	. .	John Thompson, Penrith
Second	. .	T. Robinson, Carlisle
Third	. .	J. Duckworth, Harkrigg

LIGHT WEIGHTS.

First Prize, a gold watch .	John Mason, Glencogo
Second ditto, a silver watch .	Geo. Mason, Killington
Third ditto, a silver snuff box .	M. Robinson, Kerbystephen
Fourth ditto, a silver snuff box .	Geo. Sanderson, Unthank

HEAVY WEIGHTS.

First Prize, a gold watch . . John Smith Hutton
Second ditto, a silver watch . T. Robinson, Carlisle
Third ditto, a silver snuff box . M. Robinson, Kirbystephen
Fourth ditto, a silver snuff box . J. Lagan, St. Bees

A donation of 40 guineas was presented to the two benevolent institutions of Cumberland and Westmoreland, in the names of the following gentlemen :—Messrs. T. Clemitson and F. Bell, for Cumberland ; and Messrs. R. Margetson and John Richardson, for Westmoreland.

1861.

The annual dinner was held at the " Guildhall Shades," on the 19th February, and was well attended. The Secretary read a report showing a handsome balance in the hands of the Treasurer. The usual loyal toasts were then given, and duly responded to, after which the election of officers was proceeded with, which resulted as below :—

CHAIRMAN.   TREASURER.
Mr. T. Clemitson   Mr. James Hodgson

HON. SECRETARY, Mr. Margetson

I

STEWARDS.

Mr. William Armstrong
  „   F. Bell
  „   J. Brown
  „   G. Gibson
  „   C. Little
  „   J. James
  „   J. Scott
  „   E. Stainton
  „   W. Thompson
  „   J. Thompson
  „   W. Radford

The wrestling took place at "Hornsey Wood House," on Good Friday, March 29th. The list of competitors included the very best men in England, consequently the sports were of more than ordinary interest. An immense crowd of spectators assembled to witness the wrestling, which was a very scientific display; such an array of talent had never before been witnessed in the London ring. Noble Ewbank, the best built wrestler of the day, was there; the gigantic William Jameson, the scientific Richard Wright, James Scott, the light weight champion, Ben Cooper, "Old Ben," the hero of a hundred rings, T. Rawlinson, G. Glaister, &c., were amongst the number. There were four classes of prizes this year, viz., the London prize for men under 11 stone, confined to residents in the metropolis. The all-comers' prize for men under 11 stone. The heavy weight prize for all-comers, and a prize for 16 picked men. In addition to which prizes were offered for running, high leaping, and pole-leaping. In consequence of such an elaborate programme, the sports occupied two days, commencing on Good Friday with the London 11 stone prize.

The following is the result:—

London Prize.

FOR MEN UNDER 11 STONE.

Second Round.

Stood.	Fell.
T. Nicholson	P. Leech
Alexander Scott	James Smith
William Gilchrist	Robert Atkinson
Walter Armstrong	George Sanderson
William Wilkinson	James Brunskill
J. Tiffin	John Robinson
Thomas Mein	James Taylor
J. Dixon	D. Dover
John Smith	R. Wilson

R. Atkinson was drawn against new blood in the shape of William Gilchrist, who made very short work of the old 'un. William Wilkinson and J. Brunskill made a good wrestle, resulting in favour of the former. It will be noticed also that George Sanderson fell to a new comer in this round.

Third Round.

Stood.	Fell.
John Dixon	T. Nicholson
John Smith	Alexander Scott
Jos. Tiffin	William Wilkinson
William Gilchrist	Walter Armstrong
Thomas Mein, odd man	

Jos. Tiffin knew too much for W. Wilkinson, the latter tried the buttock, but Tiffin slipped his head and threw him adroitly.

Fourth Round.

Stood.	Fell.
Thomas Mein	John Smith
John Dixon	Jos. Tiffin

William Gilchrist, odd man

The best wrestle in this round was that between Thomas Mein and John Smith; it was confidently expected by the majority of the spectators that Smith would win the head prize; however, no sooner had they got hold when Mr. Mein upset all the calculations of the House of Westmoreland by throwing Smith, in less than a twinkling, by the inside click. The cheering all round the ring was immense. Smith being quite a couple of stones heavier than his lithe little antagonist.

Fifth Round.

Stood.	Fell.
William Gilchrist	Thomas Mein

John Dixon, odd man

Final Falls.

William Gilchrist	John Dixon
John Dixon	William Gilchrist
John Dixon	William Gilchrist

In the final round Gilchrist gained the first fall, but Dixon proved too much for him, and afterwards threw him twice in succession. Gilchrist wrestled well, and had he been half-a-stone heavier, would undoubtedly have won the first prize.

HEAVY WEIGHT PRIZE.
Second Round.

Stood.	Fell.
William Jameson	M. Robinson
Tom Rawlinson	T. Nicholson
Richard Wright	D. Johnston

Stood.	Fell.
Noble Ewbank	T. Sharpe
J. Nattras	John Smith
T. Blackett	G. Glaister
Walter Armstrong	A. Wilson
J. Thompson	J. Dixon
A. Scott	W. Newman
T. Taylor	T. Whiteford

James Scott, odd man

The three champions, Jameson, Wright and Ewbank, were greeted with hearty cheers as each threw his man with the greatest ease.

Third Round.

Stood.	Fell.
James Scott	James Taylor
Benjamin Cooper	J. Nattras
Noble Ewbank	A. Scott
William Jameson	T. Blackett
J. Thompson	Walter Armstrong
Richard Wright	T. Rawlinson

Fourth Round.

Noble Ewbank	Ben Cooper
Richard Wright	J. Thompson
William Jameson	James Scott

Fifth Round.

William Jameson	Richard Wright

Noble Ewbank, odd man

Final Falls.

Noble Ewbank	William Jameson
William Jameson	Noble Ewbank
William Jameson	Noble Ewbank

In the final struggle, Noble gained the first fall, Jameson the last two. It was a fine display of strength and science, but Ewbank had to succumb to the superior weight of his opponent.

Running High Leap.

First   .   . D. Johnston, Loughstead
Tie for   } Thomas Robinson, Carlisle
Second and Third } J. Thompson, Penrith

Light-Weight Prize.

ALL COMERS—11 STONE MEN.

Second Round.

Stood.	Fell.
J. Smith	D. Johnston
Ben Cooper	Thos. Mein
M. Robinson	Jas. Scott
T. Nicholson	Jos. Gilchrist
Geo. Sanderson	Jno. Dixon

James Scott was thrown in this round very unexpectedly by Matthew Robinson. The neatest of outside chips brought the Champion light-weight on his knees, much to his chagrin. G. Sanderson lifted J. Dixon, and threw him with the hipe.

Third Round.

Stood.	Fell.
G. Sanderson	T. Nicholson
Ben Cooper	M. Robinson
Jno. Smith, odd man	

Fifth Round.

Stood.	Fell.
J. Smith	G. Sanderson
B. Cooper, odd man	

Sanderson wrestled Smith all over the ring, but weight told against him, and Smith gained the fall.

Final Falls.

Stood.	Fell.
Ben Cooper	Jno. Smith
Ben Cooper	Jno. Smith

In the final falls " Old Ben" got into his favourite
position (slack holds) each time, with his head over
Smith's shoulder, grinning that peculiar grin, which
always foretold the downfall of his antagonist. Smith
stood no chance, for Ben literally mowed him down,
and was proclaimed the winner.

16 PICKED MEN.

First Round.

Stood.	Fell.
Ben Cooper	D. Johnston
J. Milner	J. Thompson
Thos. Blackett	T. Robinson
N. Ewbank	R. Wright
T. Rawlinson	J. Smith
J. Scott	J. Nattras
G. Glaister	M. Robinson
W. Mathers	T. Sharp

The contest between Wright and Ewbank was very
interesting, each wrestled desperately; their size and
weight being about equal, made the struggle a
splendid one, which ended in a dog fall. On coming
together again Noble had the best of the tussle
throwing Wright cleverly.

Second Round.

Stood.	Fell.
Ben Cooper	J. Milner
T. Rawlinson	W. Mather
Noble Ewbank	G. Glaister
J. Scott	T. Blackett

Third Round.

T. Rawlinson	Ben Cooper
Noble Ewbank	Jas. Scott

Final Falls.

Stood.	Fell.
Tom Rawlinson	Noble Ewbank
Noble Ewbank	Tom Rawlinson
Noble Ewbank	Tom Rawlinson

The victory of Noble Ewbank was received with great cheering. His handsome appearance and gentlemanly behaviour rendered him a general favourite wherever he went.

POLE-LEAPING.

Wm. Jameson, Penrith ⎫
D. Johnston, Loughhead ⎭ Tie, 1st and 2nd
J. Robinson, Carlisle ⎫
Ben Cooper, Carlisle ⎭ Tie, 3rd and 4th

The pole-leaping was keenly contested. Jameson, in spite of his great weight, would not be denied, and succeeded in making a tie for first place with one of the best leapers of the day.

The prizes were awarded as follows:—

LONDON PRIZE.

First prize, a gold watch . . John Dixon, Kirbystephen
Second ditto, a silver watch . Wm. Gilchrist, Carlisle
Third ditto, a silver snuff-box . Thos. Mein, Burgh
Fourth ditto, a silver snuff-box Joseph Tiffin, Welton

HEAVY WEIGHTS.

First prize	£12 12	0	William Jameson, Penrith
Second ditto	6 6	0	Noble Ewbank, Bampton
Third ditto	3 3	0	Richard Wright, Longtown
Fourth ditto	3 3	0	James Scott, Carlisle
Fifth ditto	1 11	6	Walter Armstrong, Carlisle
Sixth ditto	1 11	6	J. Thompson, Penrith
Seventh ditto	1 11	6	Ben Cooper, Carlisle
Eighth ditto	1 11	6	T. Rawlinson, Wharton

11 Stone Prize, all Comers.

First prize	£8	8	0	Ben Cooper, Carlisle
Second ditto	4	4	0	John Smith, Old Hutton
Third ditto	2	2	0	George Sanderson, Unthank
Fourth ditto	2	2	0	M. Robinson, Kirbystephen
Fifth ditto	1	1	0	T. Nicholson, Carlisle
Sixth ditto	1	1	0	J. Dixon, Kirby Lonsdale
Seventh ditto	1	1	0	W. Gilchrist, Carlisle
Eighth ditto	1	1	0	James Scott, Carlisle

16 Picked Men.

First prize,	£5	0	0	Noble Ewbank, Bampton
Second ditto	2	10	0	T. Rawlinson, Wharton
Third ditto	1	5	0	James Scott, Carlisle
Fourth ditto	1	5	0	Ben Cooper, Carlisle

1862.

The Annual Dinner took place at the " Guildhall Shades," when the following officers were elected:—

CHAIRMAN,   TREASURER,
Mr. T. Clemistson   Mr. James Hodgson
HON. SECRETARY, Mr. R. Margetson
STEWARDS:
Mr. F. Bell
" Wm. Armstrong
" Wm. Thompson
" J. Thompson
" Wm. Leggett
" — Nelson
" C. Little
" George Gibson
" J. Brown
" T. Charlton
" John Smith
" J. James

The wrestling came off at " Hornsey Wood House,"

on Good Friday, April 18th, 1862. There was a large attendance of spectators, notwithstanding the counter attractions in and around London. The pole-leaping—a new feature in the sports—elicited great applause. The champion, Robert Musgrave, made his first appearance in the London Ring this year, and took the first prize; William Jameson, unwilling to be shaken off, making a tie with Baines for second place. The Umpires were Messrs. Bell and Brown. Referee, Mr. R. Margetson. The following is the result of the sports :—

The London Prize,

FOR MEN UNDER 11 STONE.

Second Round.

Stood.	Fell.
R. Brunskill	J. Dixon, Wigton
John Smith	Jos. Gilchrist
J. Robinson	R. Wilson
J. Dixon, Kirby Lonsdale	J. Baines
G. Hunton	W. Pearce
J. Tiffin	J. Foster
T. Rowe	W. Armstrong
G. Reed	J. Armstrong
G. Sanderson	J. Pugmire
Wm. Gilchrist	J. Walker

Tom Robinson, odd man

John Smith and Jos. Gilchrist had a tough wrestle. Smith missed his first stroke, intended for a finisher, when Gilchrist seized the opportunity, but the great reach of his tall adversary enabled him to

avail himself of that very old-fashioned chip, the back
heel, by which he threw Gilchrist heavily.

Third Round.

Stood.	Fell.
R. Brunskill	T. Robinson
Wm. Gilchrist	G. Hunton
G. Sanderson	J. Robinson
John Dixon	J. Tiffin
John Smith	T. Rowe

G. Reed, odd man.

A good wrestle between Tiffin and Dixon, weight
prevailing.

Fourth Round.

Stood.	Fell.
G. Sanderson	G. Reed
John Smith	R. Brunskill
John Dixon	Wm. Gilchrist

G. Sanderson threw his man in his usual scientific
style; Smith screwed Brunskill down. When J. Dixon
and W. Gilchrist stepped into the ring they were loudly
cheered. They soon succeeded in getting hold, when
Dixon won the fall by the half-buttock.

Fifth Round.

Stood.	Fell.
John Smith	George Sanderson

John Dixon, odd man.

The excitement was very great when Smith and
Sanderson came together, and a splendid wrestle was
anticipated. There was a great disparity in the size
of the men, Smith being the taller by nearly a head.
They got hold without much trouble. Smith immediately led off with the swing, but Sanderson stuck

to him like a leech, with difficulty keeping on his
feet; now he is nearly down, and the spectators
think it is all over; now he saves himself by a quick
movement, but Smith is off with him again, with the
swing, this time like lightning; again Sanderson
follows him, stops him with the inside click for an
instant, when round goes Smith again with another
swing,—mortal man could stand up no longer, and
the wiry Sanderson goes down, after making by far
the best wrestle of the day.

Final Falls.

Stood.	Fell.
John Smith	John Dixon
John Smith	John Dixon

John Dixon had no chance against the superior
weight of Smith, who threw him twice in succession,
and was declared the winner of the gold watch.

Poor Smith died of consumption on the 27th of June,
1867. His gentlemanly and unassuming conduct
won the respect of all who knew him. He was a
great favourite in the London Ring, and a good
wrestler. His first appearance in the metropolis
was at the anniversary at Hornsey Wood House, on
Good Friday, March 21st, 1856, when he succeeded
in winning the second prize for men of all weights, a
silver snuff-box. On Good Friday, 1857, he carried
off the heavy weight prize, a silver watch, throwing
the celebrated Brunskill and several other famous

wrestlers. In 1858 he was second to G. Gibson at Hackney Wick, and obtained a silver snuff-box. At the summer *fête* at the Crystal Palace, shortly afterwards, he won the all weight prize, a silver medal and purse. On the 18th of September, in the same year, at the Crystal Palace, he was invited by the Early Closing Association, and at their *fête* he won the champion's belt and purse. In the year 1860, at Hornsey Wood House, he added another to his beadrole of victories. The prize was a gold watch, value eighteen guineas. Last year he was compelled to succumb to the celebrated Ben Cooper, of Carlisle, who won the first prize, Smith taking second honours.

11-STONE PRIZE—ALL COMERS.

Second Round.

Stood.	Fell.
J. Robinson	William Wilkinson
Walter Armstrong	J. Lindsay
George Scott	J. Walker
J. Tiffin	R. Coulthard
William Armstrong	William Gilchrist
G. Sanderson	J. Baines
James Scott	J. Dixon
R. Brunskill	W. Snowdon
John Smith	R. Tyson
T. Robinson	T. Mein

H. Steel, odd man

George Scott obtained an easy victory over Walker; Tiffin surprized everybody by throwing Coulthard, who was supposed to be the coming light weight.

Third Round.

Stood.	Fell.
George Scott	H. Steel
J. Smith	T. Robinson
James Scott	George Sanderson
Walter Armstrong	J. Robinson
Willliam Armstrong	J. Tiffin
R. Brunskill odd man	

George Scott again threw his man cleverly; Tiffin made a good stand against William Armstrong, but was compelled to succumb.

Fourth Round.

Stood.	Fell.
Walter Armstrong	R. Brunskill
James Scott	J. Smith
George Scott	William Armstrong

Smith laid down to James Scott, William Armstrong fell to an outside stroke, and Brunskill to a fatal inside click.

Fifth Round.

Stood.	Fell.
George Scott	Walter Armstrong
James Scott, odd man	

The Scotts were too many for the Armstrongs; George Scott throwing the last of the clan by a good hipe, after a deal of trouble with the little 'un, who was very unwilling to be defeated.

Final Falls.

Stood.	Fell.
George Scott	James Scott
James Scott	George Scott
James Scott	George Scott

Immense excitement prevailed when the two Scotts came together for the final falls. George Scott was the stouter looking of the two, but it was thought he lacked experience to cope with the scientific wrestler who was the acknowledged champion of the light weights. James Scott was the best wrestler of his day at 11-stones; with a perfect knowledge of the art, he united a well-built frame, a sound judgment, and good temper. No man was more popular in his profession, and no wrestler gained more prizes. His unassuming manner, and the extreme neatness of his appearance in the ring, always drew forth applause from the spectators, and whenever a prize was given for neatest costume, "Bonny Jim" generally carried it off. In the final struggle for this prize his opponent gained the first fall, but in the next two wrestles the champion threw George Scott twice in succession, and was hailed the winner amidst tremendous cheering.

HEAVY WEIGHTS.

Third Round.

Stood.	Fell.
J. Blair	G. Scott
R. Wright	J. Brunskill
James Scott	C. Hutchinson
T. Rawlinson	George Sanderson
J. Brunskill	R. Tyson
William Jameson	J. Thompson
Ben Cooper	John Dixon

Rawlinson had a hard struggle to throw G. Sanderson in this round; he attempted the hipe unsuccessfully, when Sanderson clicked in the inside, and held him for the space of nearly half-a-minute; it looked anybody's fall, but Rawlinson, making a desperate effort, shook off his opponent and threw him cleverly.

Fourth Round.

Stood.	Fell.
J. Brunskill	J. Blair
William Jameson	James Scott
R. Wright	T. Rawlinson

Ben Cooper, odd man

Fifth Round.

R. Wright	Ben Cooper
W. Jameson	J. Brunskill

Final Falls.

W. Jameson	R. Wright
R. Wright	W. Jameson
W. Jameson	R. Wright

The two champions were a long time in getting their first hold; no sooner, however, was this accomplished, when Jameson lifted his man and hiped him rather easily. The next ʿwrestle was a short one; Jameson attempted to lift Wright again, when Dick made a sudden movement, and the gigantic Jameson was on his back in a second. A better throw from the breast has seldom been seen, and Jameson seemed astonished. The last fall fairly wearied out the spectators; finally, when it was getting dark, Jameson bored Wright down, and won the chief prize and the Champion's Belt.

The pole leaping claimed a large share of attention amongst the spectators, the fine and graceful style of Musgrove being much admired. He bids fair to rival the fame of his brother, who was the most celebrated leaper of his time, and will be well remembered by all lovers of the art in which he excelled.

Prize winners on Good Friday, April 18th, 1862.

THE LONDON PRIZE.

First prize, gold watch. . John Smith, Old Hutton
Second ditto, silver watch . John Dixon, Kirby Lonsdale
Third ditto, silver snuff-box . George Sanderson, Unthank
Fourth ditto, silver snuff-box William Gilchrist, Carlisle

11 STONE PRIZE—ALL COMERS.

First prize, £8 8s. . . James Scott, Carlisle
Second ditto, £4 4s. . . George Scott, Cumwhitton
Third ditto, £2 2s. . . Walter Armstrong, Carlisle
Fourth ditto, £2 2s. . William Armstrong, Carlisle
Fifth ditto, £1 1s. . . John Smith, Old Hutton
Sixth ditto, £1 1s. . . R. Brunskill, Penrith
Seventh ditto, £1 1s. . J. Tiffin, Welton
Eighth ditto, £1 1s. . John Robinson, Cotehill

ALL WEIGHTS—ALL COMERS.

First prize, £12 12s. . William Jameson, Penrith
Second ditto, £6 6s. . Richard Wright, Longtown
Third ditto, £3 3s. . . J. Brunskill, Penrith
Fourth ditto, £3 3s. . Benjamin Cooper, Carlisle
Fifth ditto, £1 11s. 6d. . T. Rawlinson, Wharton
Sixth ditto, £1 11s. 6d. . James Scott, Carlisle
Seventh ditto, £1 11s. 6d. J. Blair, Allendale
Eighth ditto, £1 11s. 6d. John Dixon, Kirby Lonsdale

K

Pole Leaping.

First prize, £3 . . . R. Musgrove, Cockermouth
Tie for
Second and Third prize, } £1 10s. { William Iameson, Penrith
James Baines, Penrith

This year a prize of one guinea was offered for the neatest costume, with the object of doing away with the rough uniform of "breeks," "grey stockings," &c., so commonly associated with rustic athletics. The prize offered, though small, had the desired effect, several of the competitors being very tastefully attired; none of them, however, came up to James Scott, of Carlisle, whose handsome figure set off his magenta shirt and white drawers to striking advantage, consequently he was adjudged the winner.

In addition to the money prizes, handsome belts, with suitable inscriptions, were presented to William Jameson and James Scott, the champions of the heavy and light weights.

Through the success of this meeting the Committee were enabled to subscribe the sum of forty guineas to the two benevolent institutions, in equal proportions of twenty guineas each. The following gentlemen were appointed to represent the same as Life Governors, viz.:—for Cumberland, Messrs. C. Little and Wm. Armstrong; for Westmoreland, Messrs. John Smith and Thomas Charlton. This wound up the proceedings of the year, which were in all respects highly creditable to the Committee of management.

1863.

The following gentlemen were elected as officers on the 11th of February at the "Guildhall Shades."

CHAIRMAN.	HON. SECRETARY.
Mr. Frank Bell	Mr. R. Margetson

TREASURER, Mr. James Hodgson

STEWARDS.

Mr. James Brown
,, William Thompson
,, C. Little
,, John Smith
,, William Armstrong
,, J. Thompson
,, John Brown
,, William Leggett
,, T. Charlton
,, J. Richardson
,, G. Gibson

The sports took place at "Hornsey Wood House," on Good Friday, April 3rd. A great concourse of spectators assembled, and the wrestling entries were larger than usual,—so much so, that it was found impossible, with the utmost exertions of the Com-

mittee, to finish the programme on Good Friday.
Consequently the wrestling for the London prize was
held over till the following day (Saturday).

Result of the sports on Good Friday :—

11 STONE PRIZE—ALL COMERS.

Third Round.

Stood.	Fell.
R. Ritson	W. Atkinson
George Scott	R. Musgrove
James Scott	T. Phillips
W. Irving	J. Thompson
J. Little	J. Smith
M. Blair	W. Snowdon
R. Tyson	W. Cooper
William Thornthwaite	Henry Ivison

Fourth Round.

W. Thornthwaite	R. Ritson
M. Blair	R. Tyson
James Scott	James Little
George Scott	W. Irving

Fifth Round.

W. Thornthwaite	J. Scott
G. Scott	M. Blair

Final Falls.

G. Scott	W. Thornthwaite
G. Scott	W. Thornthwaite

G. Scott threw Thornthwaite twice in succession,
and won the first prize and champion's belt.

ALL WEIGHTS—ALL COMERS.

Third Round.

Stood.	Fell.
William Jameson	H. Ivison
M. Blair	R. Cummings
R. Wright	W. Cooper
T. Blackett	A. Southward
W. Irving	W. Gilchrist
James Scott	G. Sanderson
J. Brunskill	W. Graham
J. Little	T. Phillips

Fourth Round.

W. Jameson	M. Blair
R. Wright	J. Little
T. Blackett	W. Irving
James Scott	J. Brunskill

Fifth Round.

W. Jameson	James Scott
R. Wright	T. Blackett

Final Falls.

W. Jameson	R. Wright
R. Wright	W. Jameson
R. Wright	W. Jameson

Wright and Jameson had about a dozen breaks away before they could get into a wrestle. At last they succeeded in getting a good hold. Jameson's must have been a very good one, for he picked Wright up and hiped him quickly. A good deal of time was wasted in the last two falls, which were gained by Wright, amidst general acclamation.

Saturday, April 4th.—There was again a large

muster of spectators to witness the wrestling for the London prize, which, in consequence of darkness setting in, could not be decided on Good Friday. There was also some shooting for a gold watch, presented by Mrs. Stones, the proprietress of the Grounds. The sports commenced with the shooting for the watch. Considerable speculation took place on the result, Messrs. Margetson and Dixon being made the favourites, while Messrs. Hodgson, Bell, Martin, and Somerville were freely supported. Mr. Dixon was the first to take the gun in hand, bringing his bird (a slow one) to book; his example was followed by Messrs. Martin and Bell, the others missing. In the second round five of them missed, and in the third round four, viz., Messrs. Milner, Atkinson, Airey, and Armstrong, who retired from the contest. The remaining gentlemen shot up their birds, and at the commencement of the seventh and last round, Mr. Dixon had to kill to win (the others having missed two each). This he accomplished amidst loud cheers. Messrs. Margetson, Somerville, Martin, and Bell tied for the money prizes, killing five each, and agreed to shoot it off, at three birds, when Mr. Margetson and Mr. Somerville killed all and divided.

The shooting being over, the traps were removed and the ring quickly formed for the more athletic sport, and the wrestling began for the London prize.

Second Round.

Stood.	Fell.
W. Stirling	R. Wilson
R. Tyson	T. Thompson
R. Ritson	J. Newton
J. Thompson	H. Cass
William Gilchrist	John Dixon
G. Lancaster	R. Bowman
R. Wetherall	Hugh Brown
G. Sanderson	J. Baines
John Smith	J. Newton
W. Irving	Walter Armstrong
R. Atkinson	J. Wilson

William Gilchrist threw his old opponent, J. Dixon, with ease by the hipe.

Third Round.

Stood.	Fell.
W. Irving	R. Tyson
R. Ritson	G. Lancaster
J. Thompson	W. Gilchrist
R. Wetherall	W. Stirling
John Smith	R. Atkinson

G. Sanderson, odd man

Wetherall threw Stirling by getting behind him and throwing him up in the air; Smith threw R. Atkinson easily.

Fourth Round.

Stood.	Fell.
W. Irving	R. Ritson
R. Wetherall	John Smith
G. Sanderson	J. Thompson

Wetherall again threw his man in the same way, much to the astonishment of everybody.

Fifth Round.

Stood.	Fell.
G. Sanderson	R. Wetherall

W. Irving, odd man

Sanderson, though a much lighter man than Wetherall, lifted him up and hiped him without a moment's delay.

Final Falls.

Stood.	Fell.
G. Sanderson	W. Irving
G. Sanderson	W. Irving

Irving, from his superior size and weight, was the favourite, though Sanderson's well-known scientific qualities as a wrestler rendered him a very formidable opponent. The first fall was gained by Sanderson, who hiped his man in a splendid fashion. In the second round Irving was again thrown easily. In consequence of some suspicious whispering having taken place amongst the partisans of Irving, the Umpires decided that he had allowed himself to be thrown, for the purpose of making bets on the result.

It would be unfair to say that Mr. Sanderson was a party to this, as Irving was apparently thrown on his merits the first time, and if he did not do his best in the last round it was his own affair. The Committee, however, cannot be blamed for the view they took of the matter, and in withholding the first and second prizes, they adopted the only course open to them. After the wrestling a meeting was held, when it was decided that the prizes should go to the next in rotation.

Prize winners on Good Friday and Saturday, April 3rd and 4th, 1863 :—

11 STONE PRIZE—ALL COMERS.

First prize, £10 and the Champion's belt. George Scott, Cum-
[whitton
Second ditto, £5 . . . . . William Thornth-. .
[waite, Brampton
Third ditto, £2 10s. . . . . James Scott, Carlisle
Fourth ditto, £2 10s. . . . . M. Blair, Allendale
Fifth ditto, £1 5s. . . . . R. Tyson, Broughton
Sixth ditto, £1 5s. . . . . J. Little, Cumwhitton
Seventh ditto, £1 5s. . . . . W. Irving, Clifton
Eighth ditto, £1 5s. . . . . Robert Ritson,
[Brough

ALL WEIGHTS.

First prize, £14 and the Champion's belt. Richard Wright,
[Longtown
Second ditto, £7 . . . . . William Jameson,
[Penrith
Third ditto, £3 10s. . . . . T. Blaskett, Orton
Fourth ditto, £3 10s. . . . . James Scott, Carlisle
Fifth ditto, £1 15s. . . . . W. Irving, Clifton
Sixth ditto, £1 15s. . . . . J. Brunskill,
[Melmerby
Seventh ditto, £1 15s. . . . . M. Blair, Allendale
Eighth ditto, £1 15s. . . . . J. Little,
[Cumwhitton

LONDON PRIZE.

First prize, a gold watch. . R. Wetherall, Carlisle
. Second ditto, a silver watch . John Smith, Old Hutton
Third ditto, a silver snuff box. Robert Ritson, Brough
Fourth ditto, a silver snuff box. J. Thompson, Penrith

The prize of one guinea for the neatest costume was awarded to Walter Armstrong, of Carlisle.

After the accounts for the year were wound up,

the sum of 40 guineas was awarded to the two
charitable institutions, in the names of Messrs. T.
Charlton and W. Thompson, for Cumberland; and
Messrs. R. Margetson and Geo. Gibson, for Westmoreland.

Messrs. R. Margetson and William Thompson
were this year appointed Vice-presidents of the
Society, and perpetual honorary members of the
Committee, with power to vote at all Committee and
other meetings for life.

1863.

On Whit-Monday, May 25th, two watches were
offered to be wrestled for at "Hornsey Wood House,"
and a great number of amateurs resident in London
intended competing for the prizes, but, to the surprise
of all, the gigantic Jameson made his appearance,
and cast a damper on the whole affair. Several
of the wrestlers refused to enter their names,
knowing they had no chance against an opponent
of . Jameson's build. A few adventurous spirits,
however, entered the lists, and at the conclusion the
result stood thus :—

First prize, a gold watch .	. William Jameson
Second ditto, a silver watch	. John Dixon
Third ditto .	. Walter Armstrong
Fourth ditto .	. Robert Ritson

Jameson also took the first prize for the pole leaping.

A gold and silver watch were also given for pigeon shooting, which resulted as below :—

| First prize, gold watch | . | . | Mr. Fowler |
| Second ditto, silver watch | . | „ | Moore |

Messrs. R. Margetson, Davis, and others, also competed.

At the Annual Dinner, held at the " Guildhall Shades," on the 14th of May, the following report of the proceedings and position of the Society was read by the Hon. Secretary, Mr. R. Margetson :—

"In presenting their annual report, your Committee feel great pleasure in congratulating the Society on its increasing prosperity, inasmuch as after giving a larger amount in prizes than was ever given on any former occasion, and, in addition, the handsome sum of forty guineas to the charitable institutions of the two counties, a balance of £100 remains at the banker's to the credit of the Society, being the largest surplus ever held since its first existence. As it is a fact not generally known to the Society at large, it may be mentioned that since the alteration in the mode of. collecting their funds was first established, the large amount of THREE HUNDRED AND FIFTY-SEVEN POUNDS has been presented to the charitable institutions of Cumberland and Westmoreland ; and when

the great benefits derived by the old and helpless of
one county, and the children of indigent parents
belonging to the other, is considered, your Committee
feel assured that this mode of disposing of the surplus, will not only meet your approbation, but that
every member of the Society will feel pleasure in the
reflection of adding his mite to the assistance of his
less fortunate fellow-countrymen.

" Whilst on this subject, your Committee deem it not
superfluous to call the attention of all natives of the
two counties to the existence of these excellent institutions, the objects of which, and the benefits they
have been the means of extending to many neces-
sitous and deserving individuals, cannot be too highly
spoken of, or too generally made known, and in
making a strong appeal on their behalf, would point
out to all young men from the two counties the pro-
priety of becoming active members as soon as they
are in a position to do so, and thus recruit the vacancies that may arise in the ranks of existing members
from death or other causes, for whilst much good has
already been effected, it is to be deplored that their
means are all too limited to provide for the numbers
of cases presenting themselves, as is evidenced by the
fact that this year there are several candidates over
and above the number of vacancies at the disposal of
each society. In concluding this report your com-
Committee would remark that they have, as your
representatives, not only important duties to perform

in the way of procuring means to carry out their promises for Good Friday, but that, independent of loss of time, it is to them an unavoidable expense, with no return or remuneration beyond the hope of giving satisfaction to the public. It must be evident, however, that anything short of this is thankless and discouraging, and equally so, that in the good-will and desire of the members themselves to do their utmost in seconding the efforts of the committee to make everything go smooth, and carry out the sports of the Society, lies the secret of their success."

1864.

The Annual General Meeting was held at the "Guildhall Shades," when the following gentlemen were elected to carry out the business of the Society:—

CHAIRMAN.	TREASURER.
Mr. Frank Bell	Mr. James Hodgson

HON. SECRETARY, Mr. William Armstrong

STEWARDS.

Mr. William Thompson
,, James Brown
,, George Gibson
,, William Leggett
,, R. Atkinson
,, C. Little
,, J. S. Brown
,, Thomas Charlton
,, Jos. Gilchrist
,, J. Richardson

The wrestling took place for the first time at the Agricultural Hall, Islington, on Good Friday, March 25th. The sports had hitherto generally been held on the green sward, the ring belted with spectators, resembling that seen on Carlisle swifts, or any other wrestling arena in the North of England. It therefore, at first sight, seemed somewhat preposterous that the large Hall at Islington which serves so many purposes throughout the year, should be selected as the place for holding a meeting of this kind. Success, however, waited upon the new " idea," for by one o'clock, the doors of the Hall were quite besieged, and upon their being opened a rush was speedily made to obtain the best positions, but so ample was the accommodation, that no difficulty whatever was experienced in obtaining seats. Soon after the commencement of the sports, the vast building was comfortably filled, and by four o'clock, the whole of the galleries surrounding the ring were closely packed by eager and excited spectators. This was the year preceding the unhappy disagreement amongst the members composing the Committee of management, who not only squandered away the whole of the surplus money (over £120), but, by their ill-advised and indiscreet bickerings, degraded the Society in the eyes of the public to such an extent, that had some improvement not taken place recently in the management of its affairs, no man of respectability would have allowed his name to be associated with it.

A donation of 40 guineas was handed to the two benevolent institutions. The sum of 20 guineas was also presented to the Warehousemen and Clerk's and Commercial Traveller's Schools, which being contrary to the rules of the Society, was the principal cause of the division amongst its members.

THE LONDON PRIZE.

Third Round.

Stood.	Fell.
James Baines	H. Atkinson
Archibald Bell	T. Jenkinson
R. Tyson	R. Atkinson
T. Holmes	G. Lancaster
R. Coulthard	T. Fawcett
R. Wetherall	W. Jackson
W. Gilchrist	T. Newton
W. Pearson	John Dixon

Fourth Round.

W. Pearson	R. Wetherall
R. Coulthard	T. Holmes
J. Baines	A. Bell
R. Tyson	W. Gilchrist

Fifth Round.

R. Coulthard	J. Baines
W. Pearson	R. Tyson

Final Falls.

R. Coulthard	W. Pearson
R. Coulthard	W. Pearson

Richard Coulthard wrestled well throughout, and decidedly proved himself the champion of the London men by winning the gold watch.

11 STONE PRIZE—ALL COMERS.

Third Round.

Stood.	Fell.
Jos. Allison	M. Mein
W. Watson	R. Musgrove
R. Blair	J. Milburn
C. Graham	G. Lancaster
James Scott	J. Tiffin
J. Dixon	W. Dixon
R. Coulthard	R. Tyson
T. Davidson	W. Pearson
J. Craig	Clem. Kennedy
A. Bell	W. Gilchrist

Fourth Round.

W. Watson	J. Craig
A. Bell	J. Dixon
T. Davidson	C. Graham
J. Allison	R. Coulthard
R. Blair	James Scott

Fifth Round.

W. Watson	A Bell
J. Allison	T. Davidson

R. Blair, odd man

Sixth Round.

W. Watson	R. Blair

J. Allison, odd man

Final Falls.

W. Watson	J. Allison
J. Allison	W. Watson
W. Watson	J. Allison

ALL WEIGHTS—ALL COMERS.

Fourth Round.

Matthew Lee	T. Robinson
A. Slack	W. Wilson
G. Maxwell	H. Ivison
M. Blair	J. Milburn
J. Whitburn	W. Glaister
J. Moses	R. Blair
J. Emmerson	L. Wilson

Fifth Round.

Stood.	Fell.
A. Slack	M. Blair
M. Lee	J. Moses
J. Emmerson	J. Whitburn

George Maxwell, odd man

Sixth Round.

G. Maxwell	A. Slack
M. Lee	J. Emmerson

Final Falls.

G. Maxwell	M. Lee
G. Maxwell	M. Lee

The celebrated champions, Wright and Jameson, were debarred by the Committee this year, in order to give the other wrestlers a better chance of gaining prizes. To debar a man because he is a good wrestler seems rather unfair, and can scarcely be considered good policy, for reasons which will be patent to all who understand and take an interest in this popular exercise.

Prize winners on Good Friday, March 25th, 1863 :—

THE LONDON PRIZE.

First prize, gold watch .	. Richard Coulthard, Cockermouth
Second ditto, silver watch	. W. Pearson, Carlisle
Third ditto, silver snuff box .	R. Tyson, Carlisle
Fourth ditto, silver snuff box	James Baines, Penrith
Fifth ditto, gold pencil case .	William Gilchrist, Carlisle
Sixth ditto, gold pencil case .	Archibald Bell, Dereham
Seventh ditto, gold pencil case	T. Holmes, Carlisle
Eighth ditto, gold pencil case	R. Wetherall, Carlisle

11-Stone Prize—All Comers.

First prize	£12	0	0	W. Watson, Weardale
Second ditto	6	0	0	Jos. Allison, Weardale
Third ditto	3	0	0	R. Blair, Allendale
Fourth ditto	3	0	0	J. Davidson, Castleside
Fifth ditto	1	10	0	A. Bell, Dereham
Sixth ditto	1	10	0	James Scott, Carlisle
Seventh ditto	1	10	0	R. Coulthard, Cockermouth
Eighth ditto	1	10	0	J. Dixon, Kirby Lonsdale

Heavy Weights—All Comers.

First prize,	£15	0	0	George Maxwell, Rockliffe
Second ditto	8	0	0	Matthew Lee, Leaprigg
Third ditto	4	0	0	J. Emmerson, Weardale
Fourth ditto	4	0	0	A. Slack, Skirwith
Fifth ditto	2	0	0	J. Whitburn, Barrow
Sixth ditto	2	0	0	J. Moses, Cockermouth
Seventh ditto	2	0	0	M. Blair, Allendale
Eighth ditto	2	0	0	L. Wilson, Egremont

Pole-Leaping.

First prize	£5	0	0	R. Musgrove, Keswick
Second ditto	2	10	0	James Baines, Penrith
Third ditto	1	10	0	W. Pearson, Carlisle
Fourth ditto	1	0	0	G. Maxwell, Rockliffe

Steeplechase.

First prize	£2	10	0	R. Musgrove, Keswick
Second ditto	1	10	0	G. Maxwell, Rockliffe
Third ditto	1	0	0	T. Robinson, Carlisle

The prize for the neatest costume was divided between Walter Armstrong, Carlisle, and Archibald Bell, Dereham.

1864.

On the 6th of August, prizes were offered for 9½ stone men, and men of all weights, at Cremorne Gardens. The meeting was well attended, and the wrestlers mustered in great force, more especially the lighter division, a number of whom (11 stone men) brought themselves down to mere shadows so as to compete for the feather weight prize. The wrestling was keenly contested, and resulted as below :—

MEN UNDER 9½ STONE.

First Prize, a gold watch	.	George Sanderson
Second ditto, a silver watch	.	Walter Armstrong
Third, no prize	. .	Richard Tyson

ALL WEIGHTS.

First prize, gold watch	.	Richard Coulthard
Second ditto, a silver watch	.	John Thompson
Third, no prize	. .	Thos. Robinson

The pole leaping was won by James Baines

In the heavy weights, Thompson threw Robinson cleverly, and when he stood up with R. Coulthard to contend for the head prize, he looked like winning, being much stronger than his opponent. Coulthard, however, threw him twice in succession, and was declared the winner. Walter Armstrong threw Tyson (in the feathers) one of the 11 stone " shadows." Then came the final falls with Geo. Sanderson. W. Armstrong gained the first fall, and Sanderson the last two, who was hailed the victor amidst loud applause.

1865.

On the 7th of June, 1864, the Annual Dinner of the Society took place at the "Guildhall Shades," when the officers for the ensuing year were elected as below:—

CHAIRMAN.	TREASURER.
Mr. Frank Bell	Jas. Hodgson.

HON. SECRETARY, Wm. Armstrong.

STEWARDS.

Mr. Wm. Thompson
 „ J. Brown
 „ G. Gibson
 „ C. Little
 „ R. Atkinson
 „ J. S. Brown
 „ Jos. Wills
 „ W. Jameson
 „ Jos. Richardson

On the approach of the Annual General Meeting, a rumour gained currency that exception would be taken to the conduct of the officers who had the control of the affairs of the Society. The first meeting of the subscribers was held at the "Guildhall Shades," Gresham-street, when there was a very full attendance. Mr. Frank Bell officiated as Chairman, supported by Messrs. James Hodgson (Treasurer), William Armstrong (Hon. Sec.), Thompson, Leggett, Margetson, Brown, Little, Atkinson, &c. In opening the proceedings, Mr. Bell adverted to the rumour which he said was flying about, and remarked that he understood a "hole and corner meeting" had been held with the object of turning the present Committee out of office. Messrs. Margetson and Leggett both rose to order, but the Chairman interposed, by saying that he was now quite prepared to proceed with the more immediate business of the meeting. Mr. William Armstrong disclaimed any connection with clandestine meetings, he attended fearlessly in his capacity of Secretary, to lay before the members his accounts for 1864, which he felt confident would prove satisfactory. Mr. Gilchrist opposed the adoption of the accounts, on the ground that the funds had not been carefully or properly expended, and that the rules had been violated by giving douceurs to the Warehousemen and Clerks' and Commercial Travellers Schools. Mr. William Armstrong then informed the company that there was a balance of £123 13s. 11d. in hand, and produced the voucher. Mr. Margetson said he did not wish to create any dissension, but any member of the Society had a perfect right to take exception to any item of expenditure if he thought the same inconsistent and in violation of the rules of the Association. Mr. Margetson continued :—it was essentially necessary to have a permanent Committee. Their experience in former years must convince every one that the business of the Society would never be successfully managed until this reform was brought about. It must be well known to those who were acquainted with the rules, that they had been violated in granting 20 guineas to the above-named schools. They were deserving institutions, but not more so than others, children were well known to be increasing as applicants in the Westmoreland schools, and this year the candidates were far in excess of the vacancies at the disposal of that institution. This was the legitimate channel for the surplus funds. Mr. Charlton moved a vote of want of confidence in the Committee. Mr. Westmoreland objected to the motion, a fortnight's notice must be given. Eventually no motion was put, and the meeting broke up.

A second meeting was held at the same place, on Wednesday, March the 8th. Mr. Frank Bell occupying the chair. After a stormy discussion Mr. Charlton again moved a vote of want of confidence in the Committee, which was seconded by Mr. Mein, and unanimously carried. The three chief officers, Chairman, Secretary, and Treasurer were then summarily voted out, and finally Mr. Leggett was elected Chairman. At a subsequent meeting held under the presidency of the newly-elected Chairman, the following gentlemen formed themselves into a Committee.

CHAIRMAN.   HON. SEC.

Mr. Wm. Leggett   R. Margetson

TREASURER, Jos. Gilchrist.

Each Committee continued to hold meetings up to Good Friday. The old Committee, headed by Mr. Frank Bell, advertising their wrestling to come off at Cremorne Gardens, while the other, under the presidency of Mr. Leggett, announced their sports to take place at the Agricultural Hall, consequently two meetings would be held on the same day.

GOOD FRIDAY AT THE AGRICULTURAL HALL.

A very large company assembled at the Agricultural Hall, and, to judge from the number of spectators, it would scarcely have been thought that another display of the same kind was taking place in the metropolis. The sports commenced with a hurdle race between twelve competitors, in a series of heats, which was won by T. Sedgwick, T. Sanders second, J. Marshall third. The real business of the day then began, the hurdle race merely playing the prelude to the more exciting contests that were to follow.

WRESTLING FOR THE LONDON PRIZE.
Second Round.

Stood.	Fell.
W. Marshall	C. Donald
W. Gilchrist	J. Dinwoode
R. Ritson	H. Brown
R. Brown	James Murray
Thomas Mein	J. Pattinson
J. Graham	R. Brown
R. Fawcett	W. Thompson
J. Thompson	R. Wetherall
R. Tyson	G. Beatty
James Edgar	A. Robinson
Walter Armstrong	J. Hilton
Robert Atkinson	E. Wilson
Thomas S. Sedgwick	J. Graham
G. Hunter	J. Marshall

Third Round.

J. Thompson	R. Brown
James Edgar	R. Fawcett
G. Hunton	W. Marshall
J. Graham	R. Atkinson
William Gilchrist	Thomas Mein
Walter Armstrong	R. Ritson
T. Sedgwick	R. Tyson

Fourth Round.

T. Sedgwick	J. Graham
Walter Armstrong	J. Thompson
G. Hunton	W. Gilchrist

J. Edgar, odd man

Fifth Round.

James Edgar	T. Sedgwick
Walter Armstrong	G. Hunton

Final Falls.

James Edgar	Walter Armstrong
James Edgar	Walter Armstrong

The excitement as the last pair entered the arena

was very great, and they were loudly cheered. The superior height and weight of Edgar gave him a great advantage, and he succeeded in backheeling his opponent each time. The first prize was therefore taken by Jas. Edgar, the second by Walter Armstrong, the third by Geo. Hunter, &c. The pole-leaping next commenced, which was won by R. Musgrove, having also taken the prize at the Cremorne meeting only a few hours previously. P. Winder was second.

WRESTLING FOR MEN UNDER 11 STONE—ALL COMERS.

Third Round.

Stood.	Fell.
J. Graham	R. Musgrove
J. Allison	R. Ritson
James Scott	William Gilchrist
Henry Ivison	W. Moffatt
Jos. Dixon	S. Hewitson
Clem. Kennedy	G. Sanderson
J. Nattras	J. Thompson

R. Tyson, odd man

Fourth Round.

J. Nattras	J. Dixon
J. Allison	Clem. Kennedy
Henry Ivison	R. Tyson
James Scott	J. Graham

Fifth Round.

James Allison	J. Nattras
James Scott	Harry Ivison

Final Falls.

James Scott	Jos. Allison
Jos. Allison	James Scott
Jos. Allison	James Scott

Some splendid wrestling took place in this

competition. The first two rounds weeded out the inferior men; then followed a display of scientific skill that elicited the heartiest applause from the vast assembly. The final round brought together the celebrated James Scott, of Carlisle, and Jos. Allison, of Wardale—a wrestler who, to greater weight and strength, had also youth in his favour. Despite these advantages, he was thrown cleverly in the first bout. In the second Allison got the best hold, and threw Scott over his knee. Scott tried to lift his man in the last fall, and slipping, was bored down. Allison was, therefore, declared the winner amidst loud cheers; Scott was also warmly applauded for the gallant struggle he had made.

All Weight Wrestling—All Comers.

Third Round.

Stood.	Fell.
J. Thompson	J. Pattinson
George Maxwell	G. Sanderson
James Edgar	J. Dixon
Jos. Allison	J. Graham
Walter Armstrong	Clem. Kennedy
James Scott	J. Little
John Mitchell	J. Emmerson

J. Nattras, odd man

Fourth Round.

James Scott	James Edgar
J. Mitchell	Jos. Allison
J. Thompson	G. Maxwell
J. Nattras	Walter Armstrong

Fifth Round.

Stood.	Fell.
J. Nattras	J. Thompson
John Mitchell	James Scott

Final Falls.

John Mitchell	J. Nattras
John Mitchell	J. Nattras

Never in the recollection of the oldest frequenters of the wrestling were so many exciting contests witnessed as took place for this prize, and never were the professionals so utterly defeated by amateurs as on this day. In the second round J. Thompson, an amateur, threw Matthew Lee, the Lyneside champion; the spectators were amazed when they saw the giant's heels cleave the air to the tune of a cross-buttock. In the fourth round Thompson also threw George Maxwell, who won the heavy weight prize at the last annual meeting. The prowess of John Mitchell, however, principally interested the spectators; he commenced by throwing Harry Ivison in the second round. The next man who fell to him was J. Emerson, of Weardale. Jos. Allison of Weardale, came next, who made a splendid effort to throw Mitchell; Allison's legs bent and quivered beneath him, but it seemed as if he might as well have tried to upset the monument, and when his strength was exhausted, Mitchell threw him like a child. As the struggle of the heavy weights drew to a close, it was watched with increased interest; after the fourth round the contest lay between J. Mitchell, Thompson, James Scott, and J. Nattras. The struggle between Nattras ,and Thompson was a long one, but eventually Nattras gained the fall. Mitchell and Scott then came together, and a splendid wrestle ensued, but all the science of the brilliant light was as nothing in the face of Mitchell's over-powering strength, and he too went down. Then came the final two out of three between Mitchell and Nattras. Both men were pretty well blown — Mitchell apparently the most so—his great bulk causing a difficulty in his breathing, whilst his tall, wiry, active antagonist seemed far freer from signs of over-exertion. After a brief rest they went at it amidst the cheers of the audience, which stood in breathless anxiety, awaiting the result. A good deal of finessing, and they closed; a tremendous effort on each side followed, and in a second, a shout rent the air,—" Nattras is felled ! " The excitement was now "piled up " by the next wrestle ending in a dog fall —the decision of the referee being loudly applauded —and the round was resumed, when Mitchell obtained the fall by a cross-buttock. The winner was loudly cheered, and was carried in triumph round the arena.

The winners of the principal prizes during the day were London men; this gave an *éclat* to the contests

which has been seldom equalled, and could scarcely
be surpassed.

Walter Armstrong took the prize for neatest
costume.

The prizes were awarded as below :—

THE LONDON PRIZE.

First prize, gold watch, £15 6s.	James Edgar
Second ditto, silver watch, £7.	Walter Armstrong
Third ditto, silver snuff box, £5 15s.	George Hunton
Fourth ditto, silver snuff box, £5 15s.	T. Sedgwick
Fifth ditto, silver snuff box, £3 5s.	Wm. M. Gilchrist
Sixth ditto, silver snuff box, £3 5s.	John Thompson
Seventh ditto, silver snuff box £2 16s.	John Graham
Eighth diito, silver snuff box, £2 15s.	R. Tyson

11 STONE COUNTRY PRIZES—ALL COMERS.

First prize, silver cup and £10	Jos. Allison
Second ditto, £8	James Scott
Third ditto, £3 10s.	Harry Ivison
Fourth ditto, £3 10s.	John Nattras
Fifth ditto, £2	John Graham
Sixth ditto, £2	R. Tyson
Seventh ditto, £2	Clem. Kennedy
Eighth ditto, £2	Jos. Dixon

ALL WEIGHTS—ALL COMERS.

First prize, silver cup and £8	John Mitchell
Second ditto, £8	John Nattras
Third ditto, £4	James Scott
Fourth ditto, £4	John Thompson
Fifth ditto, £2 10s.	Walter Armstrong
Sixth ditto, £2 10s.	George Maxwell
Seventh ditto, £2 10s.	Jos. Allison
Eighth ditto, £2 10s.	James Edgar
Ninth ditto, £1 10s.	J. Emmerson
Tenth ditto, £1 10s.	J. Graham
Eleventh ditto, £1 10s.	Jos. Little
Twelfth ditto, £1 10s.	C. Kennedy
Thirteenth ditto, £1 10s.	J. Irving
Fourteenth ditto, £1 10s.	Jos. Dixon
Fifteenth ditto, £1 10s.	J. Pattinson

Hurdle Race.

First prize, £3	T. Sedgwick
Second ditto, £1 10s. . . .	T. Saunders
Third ditto, 10s.	J. Marshall

Pole Leaping.

First prize, £5	R. Musgrove
Second ditto, £2 10s. . . .	P. Winder
Third ditto, £1 10s. . . .	T. Sedgwick
Fourth ditto, 10s. . . .	J. Jackson

Neatest Costume.

Walter Armstrong, £1 1s.

THE WRESTLING AT CREMORNE.

The wrestling held here was one of the conse-
quences of the "split" in the Society. It was
arranged that the sports should come off in the park
adjoining Ashburnham Hall, which was certainly a
very suitable place; but an unhappy change in the
weather on the morning of Good Friday necessitated
an alteration in this part of the programme. The
rain pouring down in torrents all the morning, the
attendance of spectators was limited, and the first
part of the competition was, to some extent, spirit-
less. There might be about two thousand persons
present, some of them under the covering of um-
brellas, while others were content to crouch under
the very indifferent shelter of tavern tables. The
proceedings were opened by a hurdle race twice
round the circle, which was won by R. Musgrove;
Archibald Bell second. The prize for pole leaping

was also won by Musgrove; James Baines second, William Jameson third. Then came the wrestling by the London residents. Some of the contests were remarkably good, the wrestling of A. Bell being especially admired. The exceeding cool and business-like style of S. Hewetson also attracted general attention, and he was loudly cheered at the close, when the wrestlers stood thus :—

First—Archibald Bell
Second—John Thompson
Third—S. Hewetson

The next prize was for men of all weights, but Jameson was the only heavy weight present. The champion at each encounter threw his comparatively puny opponents like toys and set them on their legs again almost before they knew what had befallen them. In the final falls he threw Joseph Whitehead twice in succession, and was proclaimed the winner.

The last event in the programme was the competition for the 11 stone prize, all comers. Nothing of any interest occurred until J. Milburn and R. Coulthard stood up for the final falls; the struggle was very exciting, resulting in favour of Coulthard, whose victory was hailed with much cheering. The final rounds were not concluded till after nightfall, yet, despite the depressing effects of the rain, the majority of the spectators stayed till the last.

1866.

That portion of the members who were called the New Society, held their first meeting at the " Salutation Hotel," Newgate-street, on the 31st of January, .when the statement of accounts was read by the Hon. Secretary, Mr. Margetson, shewing a balance of nearly £80 on the wrong side, to be paid by the Committee. The officers for the year were appointed, and everything put in readiness for the coming anniversaary on Good Friday. The Cremorne party held their meeting on the following Monday, at St. James's Hall, Richard Thwaites, Esq., in the chair. After referring to the unhappy differences which existed between the divided Societies, and hoping that they would again become united, the Chairman called upon the Secretary, Mr. William Armstrong, to read the report, which stated that £105 had been given in prizes last year, and the total receipts were £225 17s. 11d.; the balance in hand after all expenses were paid was £29 3s. Mr. Margetson, the representative of the Agricultural Hall party, said, he came there with a friendly feeling towards the Society for; which he had worked forty years, and nothing would please him better than to see the members united again on Good Friday. He must say, the division among them was not creditable. Nothing definite, however, was arranged till the 12th of February, when the amalgamation took place under the presidency of Mr. Margetson. Mr. James Hodgson retained his post as treasurer, and Mr. Jos. Gilchrist was elected Hon. Secretary. The Committee numbered twenty-nine.

The sports took place under the united management, at the Agricultural Hall, on Good Friday, March 30, in the presence of nearly 10,000 spectators. The sinews of war, which had suffered so severely from the split, were substantially renewed, and after paying all expenses, and clearing off the debt incurred the previous year, the Society retained a balance of £74 4s. 6d. to be carried on to the next year's account. The sports were highly appreciated, the wrestling being exceedingly good. The two northern counties sent their best men,—Wright, Jameson, Scott, Allison, Lawson, Milburn, &c., for the wrestling, and the light and agile Musgrove for the pole leaping.

The sports commenced shortly before two o'clock with the wrestling, by men not exceeding 9½ stones in weight.

9½ STONE PRIZE—ALL COMERS.
Second Round.

Stood.	Fell.
P. Winder	J. Walker
John Graham	J. Carruthers
R. Carruthers	J. Graham
George Sanderson	J. Harrison

M

Stood.	Fell.
J. Briggs	W. Parker
J. Hope	J. Fawcett
R. Irving	W. Allen
H. Taylor	T. Anderson
J. Ward	W. Armstrong

Third Round.

J. Briggs	H. Taylor
G. Sanderson	P. Winder
R. Carruthers	John Ward
John Graham	R. Irving

J. Hope, odd man

The tussle between R. Carruthers and John Ward was fiercely contested; Carruthers was nearly down two or three times, but, recovering himself each time, he at last managed to inside click his man, in a most dexterous manner, and laid him flat on his back.

Fourth Round.

Stood.	Fell.
J. Graham	J. Hope
J. Briggs	R. Carruthers

G. Sanderson, odd man

Carruthers, in trying to mend his hold with Briggs, made a slip, when his opponent, taking advantage of the same, dashed in and back-heeled him, throwing the feather-weight champion cleverly.

Fifth Round.

Stood.	Fell.
John Graham	G. Sanderson

J. Briggs, odd man

Final Falls.

John Graham	J. Briggs
John Graham	J. Briggs

John Graham wrestled with great judgment, and displayed an amount of science somewhat extraordinary in so young a wrestler, Some of his falls were worthy of the best days of Scott. In the first round, he treated Briggs to a swinging hipe, throwing him easily. In the next hold, Briggs made an attempt to lift his man, but Graham clicked him down, without falling himself, and was hailed the winner.

A hurdle race round the arena, over six flights of hurdles three feet high, was the next event, which was won easily by R. Musgrove, J. Williams, Keswick, being second.

Wrestling for the Agricultural Hall Cup, presented to the Society by Thomas Rudkin, Esq., and other prizes, by the London residents under 11 stones.

Third Round.

Stood.	Fell.
J. Wright	R. Atkinson
William Gilchrist	J. Hope
William Armstrong	G Graham
T. Saunders	J. Sanderson
G. Sanderson	J. Cartner
G. Lancaster	Geo. Hunton
John Graham	J. Thompson
R. Coulthard	James Edgar

In this round the veteran Robert Atkinson received his *coup de grace*, and fell, as old men will, before a younger and stronger man. John Graham, the winner of the 9½ stone prize, threw J. Thompson in a highly graceful manner. The winners at Cremorne and Agricultural Hall of last year, came together; the wrestle ended very unsatisfactorily, both men claimed the fall, which looked very much like a "dog" one ; but, after a consultation, the award was given to Coulthard.

Fourth Round.

Stood.	Fell.
R. Coulthard	William Gilchrist
William Armstrong	J. Wright
T. Saunders	G. Lancaster
John Graham	G. Sanderson

W. Bowerbank, odd man

George Sanderson was suffering from a wounded finger, and lost his hold; consequently, John Graham gained the fall without a struggle.

Fifth Round.

Stood.	Fell.
William Armstrong	William Bowerbank
T. Saunders	R. Coulthard

John Graham, odd man

Saunders, to the surprise of everyone, threw Coulthard very cleverly.

Sixth Round.

Stood.	Fell.
John Graham	T. Saunders

William Armstrong, odd man

The wrestling by John Graham against the vanquisher of Coulthard, was by far the cleverest of the day. Saunders was a good stone and a half the heavier man, and a very awkward customer for any one to cope with, more especially for a man of our little champion's size. No sooner had they got hold, when Saunders put in the hank; Graham, however, knew how to meet this very formidable chip. Instead of allowing himself to be pulled back, he bent forward, jerked his leg out of the hank, and crossed Saunders in a twinkling, making a splendid fall. After this performance, Graham was hailed with repeated ovations.

Final Falls.

Stood.	Fell.
John Graham	Wm. Armstrong
Wm. Armstrong	John Graham
John Graham	Wm. Armstrong

A most exciting struggle between the two men. Graham gained the first fall, after being swung round twice, Armstrong gained the second by sheer strength. In the final fall, Graham brought Armstrong down by a beautiful outside stroke. The clever young champion was immediately surrounded by his friends, and carried high around the arena, the cheering of the spectators lasting several minutes. The wrestling of John Graham was the theme of general admiration, and cannot be too highly praised, and when it is taken into consideration that he only weighed 9 stones and a half, there can be no doubt that his performance was the very first of the meeting, and has never been surpassed in the London Ring.

A grand display of pole-leaping here took place, R. Musgrove was first, clearing 10ft. 6in. P. Winder and J. Baines tied at 10ft. 3in.; Wm. Jameson retired after clearing 9ft.

WRESTLING BY MEN UNDER 11 STONE—ALL COMERS.

Third Round.

Stood.	Fell.
J. Scott	G. Sanderson
W. Lawson	R. Richardson
C. Kennedy	R. Carruthers
H. Ivison	John Ward
J. Milburn	J. Thompson

J. Allison, odd man

Fourth Round.

J. Milburn	W. Lawson
H. Ivison	G. Maxwell (over weight)
Jos. Allison	C. Kennedy

Jas. Scott, odd man

Fifth Round.

J. Milburn	H. Ivison
Jas. Scott	Jos. Allison

Final Falls.

J. Milburn	Jas. Scott
Jas. Scott	J. Milburn
J. Milburn	J. Scott

John Milburn, accordingly, won the first prize and the belt.

ALL WEIGHTS—ALL COMERS.

Fifth Round.

Stood.	Fell.
Wm. Jameson	H. Ivison
R. Wright	Jas. Edgar
Wm. Armstrong	J. Ward
J. Emmerson	J. Wilson
J. Allison	J. Milburn

Sixth Round.

Stood.	Fell.
J. Emmerson	J. Allison
Wm. Jameson	Wm. Armstrong
R. Wright	Jas. Scott

Seventh Round.

Wm. Jameson	J. Emmerson

R. Wright, odd man

Final Falls.

Wm. Jameson	R. Wright
R. Wright	Wm. Jameson
R. Wright	Wm. Jameson

A deal of time was expended in getting hold, the audience the while manifesting great impatience. At last they grappled each other, and, amid the hoarse murmurs of the spectators, many of whom crowded in upon the competitors, the struggle commenced. Jameson having the best of the hold, soon got his man into difficulties, and brought Wright to the earth with a thud. In the second fall, Jameson succeeded in "gathering" Wright, and it seemed all over with him, but Dick made a sudden leap to the ground, twisted his burly antagonist quickly round, and threw him in a most scientific manner by a stroke from the right leg. In the final fall Jameson again got the best hold but Wright declined being bored down, and without waiting for such a catastrophe, whirled Jameson cleverly upon his back by a half-buttock, thus winning the heavy weight prize. This terminated the sports, which were not concluded till a late hour.

The prizes were awarded as follows :—

9½ STONE MEN.

First prize	£5	0	0	John Graham, Carlisle
Second ditto	3	0	0	J. Briggs, Ulverstone
Third ditto	2	0	0	G. Sanderson, Unthank
Fourth ditto	1	0	0	R. Carruthers, Cumwhitton

London Prize.

11 STONE MEN.

First prize, silver cup and £3 .	John Graham, Carlisle
Second ditto, gold watch . . .	Wm. Armstrong, Keswick
Third ditto, silver snuff box . .	Thos. Saunders, Penrith
Fourth ditto, a silver snuff box .	R. Coulthard, Cockermouth
Fifth ditto, a silver snuff box . .	W. Bowerbank, Penrith
Sixth ditto, a silver snuff box . .	G. Sanderson, Unthank
Seventh ditto, a silver snuff box .	J. Wright, Longtown
Eighth ditto, a silver snuff box .	G. Lancaster, Carlisle

11 STONE MEN—ALL COMERS.

First prize, belt and £8	0	0	J. Milburn, Weardale
Second ditto	5	0	0	James Scott, Carlisle
Third ditto	3	0	0	H. Ivison, ditto
Fourth ditto	3	0	0	Jos. Allison, Weardale
Fifth ditto	2	0	0	C. Kennedy, Stapleton
Sixth ditto	2	0	0	Wm. Lawson, Newburgh
Seventh ditto	1	0	0	R. Carruthers, Cumwhitton
Eighth ditto	1	0	0	J. Thompson
Ninth ditto	1	0	0	R. Richardson
Tenth ditto	1	0	0	John Ward

ALL WEIGHTS—ALL COMERS.

First prize, belt and £10	0	0	R. Wright, Longtown
Second ditto	6	0	0	Wm. Jameson, Penrith
Third ditto	4	0	0	J. Emmerson, Weardale
Fourth ditto	2	10	0	Jos. Allison, ditto
Fifth ditto	2	10	0	J. Scott, Carlisle
Sixth ditto	2	10	0	Wm. Armstrong, Keswick
Seventh ditto	1	10	0	J. Wilson
Eighth ditto	1	10	0	J. Ward
Ninth ditto	1	10	0	J. Edgar
Tenth ditto	1	10	0	J. Milburn
Eleventh ditto	1	10	0	H. Ivison

Pole Leaping.

First prize £5 0 0 . R. Musgrove, Keswick
Second ditto 2 0 0 ⎫ Tie ⎰ P. Winder, ditto
Third ditto 2 0 0 ⎭ ⎱ James Baines, Penrith

Hurdle Race.

First prize, £3 0 0 . R. Musgrove
Second ditto 1 0 0 . J. Williams

Bell Race.

First prize £1 10 0 . John Ward
Second ditto 0 15 0 . G. Maxwell
Third ditto 0 10 0 . R. Carruthers
Fourth ditto 0 5 0 . R. Musgrove

Neatest Costume.

Richard Wright . £0 10 6
Matthew Mein . 0 10 6

1867.

The following gentlemen were elected as Stewards at the Annual General Meeting, which took place at the " Salutation Hotel," Newgate-street, on Wednesday the 6th of March.

CHAIRMAN.   TREASURER.
Mr. R. Margetson.   Mr. Thomas Mein.

HON. SECRETARY.—Mr. Jos. Gilchrist.

STEWARDS.

Mr. Thomas Baty
,, A. Bell
,, S. Hewitson
,, J. Illingworth
,, Ed. Stainton
,, G. Tomlinson
,, Jos. Wright
,, James Hodgson
,, William Little
,, Joseph Dixon
,, P. Twentyman
,, A. Scott
,, Jos. Wills
,, John Mitchell

At a subsequent meeting, Mr. Margetson having resigned his position as Chairman. Mr. William Leggett was promoted to that position, and Major Wills was appointed to the Vice-chair, in the room of Mr. Leggett.

GOOD FRIDAY AT THE AGRICULTURAL HALL.

The sports commenced between one and two o'clock. The first event on the programme was the "London Prize," by men under 11 stone. In the first round some very exciting struggles took place, which at once roused the enthusiasm of the spectators. The wrestle between John Mitchell, the champion of the heavy weights in 1865, and Thomas Graham, was well contested. The first hold ended in a "dog fall," but on renewing the round, Graham threw his man very cleverly. The men who entered for the heavy weights were splendid samples of the bone and sinew of the North of England. All who looked on the proceedings and noted the good humour which prevailed, spent an afternoon of genuine pleasure. That this northern pastime is greatly on the increase, and promises to be still more fully developed, is evidenced by the increase in the number of spectators who flock to the Agricultural Hall each year. Great changes have taken place in the public mind of late years with respect to physical training, and it is to be hoped that this very desirable accomplishment will become more general ; no other athletic exercise so thoroughly brings every muscle into play, and in a rough encounter nothing will serve a man in such good stead as a knowledge of the inside click and the cross-buttock. A Londoner was once heard to remark that nothing frightened him so much as getting *amongst the feet* of a north-countryman.

The best fall of the day was that between J. Tomlinson and John Graham, the latter treating the spectators to a cross-buttock of the real Jimmy Scott pattern. The veteran Robert Atkinson again made his appearance, and was loudly cheered when he threw his first opponent by the " back-heel."

LONDON PRIZE—FOR MEN UNDER 11 STONE.

Second Round.

Stood.	Fell.
Thomas Moffatt	R. Ritson
W. Dixon	J. Williams
Walter Armstrong	Thomas Graham
Matthew Mein	Robert Atkinson
T. Bell	C. Wills
J. Thompson	John Wilson
R. Tomlinson	Thomas Waugh
James Edgar	R. Moffatt
J. Wright	J. Pattinson
Jos. Dixon	George Sanderson
John Graham	R. Coulthard (not present)

Jos. Peel, odd man

Old Robert Atkinson made a rush at Matthew Mein, apparently intending to bore the young 'un down, but Matthew very carefully steadied himself with the click for an instant, "gathered" his man well, and hiped him, making a very clean fall of the old 'un.

Third Round.

Stood.	Fell.
T. Moffat	J. Peel
W. Dixon	W. Armstrong
Matthew Mein	T. Bell
J. Thompson	R. Tomlinson
James Edgar	J. Wright
John Graham	Jos. Dixon

J. Wright made a good wrestle with James Edgar, trying all he knew; the latter, however, had received a very liberal education in the art of wrestling, and succeeded in throwing his opponent by the swinging hipe. John Graham, by a skilful manœuvre, pulled Jos. Dixon on to his knees.

Fourth Round.

Stood.	Fell.
Thomas Moffatt	W. Dixon
J. Thompson	M. Mein
John Graham	J. Edgar

Edgar's swinging hipe would not do for John Graham, who stopped it easily, and twisted Edgar down.

Fifth Round.

Stood.	Fell.
J. Thompson	T. Moffatt

John Graham, odd man.

Thompson and Moffatt soon got hold, when Moffatt tried the hipe, and was throwing his man beautifully, but just before reaching the ground Thompson turned himself, making a dog fall. Loud cries were raised that Moffatt had won, the referee however ordered them to wrestle over again, when the result was another dog fall. Again they got hold, Thompson eventually gaining the fall.

Final Falls.

Stood.	Fell.
John Graham	J. Thompson
John Thompson	J. Graham
John Graham	J. Thompson

Graham gained the first fall by the half-buttock. In the second trial Thompson swung his man, throwing him well. Each having gained a fall, the excitement was very great, Graham's friends crowding round him to give him advice. The clever little champion, however, wanted none, for as soon as the pair got hold, he coolly cross-clicked his opponent, never allowing him to have a chance. John Graham thus won the London prize two years in succession.

Next came the hurdle race, which was again won by Robert Musgrove, J. Williams being second.

ALL WEIGHTS—ALL COMERS.
Third Round.

Stood.	Fell.
J. Collins	T. Moffatt
J. Snowden	Jos. Dixon
R. Wright	R. Tomlinson
W. Jameson	W. Armstrong
Jos. Allison	J. Allison
W. Timperton	S. King
William Armstrong	J. Edgar

Fourth Round.

Stood	Fell
J. Snowdon	J. Collins
William Jameson	R. Wright
Jos. Allison	W. Timperton
William Armstrong, odd man	

Jameson threw Wright by the inside click, after a severe struggle, thus reducing the result to a certainty.

Fifth Round.

Stood.	Fell.
William Jameson	Jos. Allison
William Armstrong	J. Snowdon .

The second wrestle was the best of the day, and the vast arena rang with the acclamations of the spectators as William Armstrong, an amateur, threw Snowdon by a superb hipe.

Final Falls.

Stood.	Fell.
William Jameson	William Armstrong
William Armstrong	William Jameson
William Jameson	William Armstrong

Loud cheers greeted the men as they stood up for the final falls. They soon got into holds, and Jameson was about to lift his man when the latter attempted to buttock the champion, but Jameson threw his weight forward, and screwed him down The result of the second round was unlooked for; as soon as they got hold, Armstrong turned in the buttock, and, amid oft-renewed cheers, brought the giant down. The last fall was a foregone conclusion. It was evident to the spectators that the champion was on his mettle, and that Armstrong's chance was a very poor one. Jameson's favourite chip is the cross buttock, which his extraordinary size and strength enables him to use in a different manner from any other wrestler; instead of turning "in," as a lighter man would have to do, he, by main strength, drags his opponent on to his own (Jameson's) back with such terrific force, that the rebound is generally enough to settle him. In this

way he threw Armstrong ; Jameson drew him up as
if he had been a child, and buttocked him high in
the air, and thus won the champion's prize. Jameson
was very good humoured at being thrown, and
appeared to think it was rather good fun, but in the
final wrestle he certainly looked in earnest.

Pole Leaping.

John Allison, of Kendal, divided the first prize
with Musgrove, who broke the cross bar at 10 ft. 3
in.; James Baines was third.

11 STONE MEN—ALL COMERS.

Third Round.

Stood.	Fell.
J. Edgar	R. Moffatt
J. Graham	J. Wright
J. Snowdon	Walter Armstrong
Jos. Allison	J. Harrison
James Scott	George Sanderson
J. Milburn	J. Collins

Fourth Round.

James Edgar	John Graham
Jos. Allison	J. Snowdon
J. Milburn	J. Scott

Fifth Round.

J. Edgar	Jos. Allison

J. Milburn, odd man

Final Falls.

J. Milburn	J. Edgar
J. Milburn	J. Edgar

Milburn threw Edgar twice in succession, and
won.

On the following day the prizes were awarded as follows:—

THE LONDON PRIZE.

First prize, silver cup and £5 . John Graham
Second ditto, gold watch . . J. Thompson
Third ditto, silver watch . . Thomas Moffatt
Fourth ditto, silver snuff box . James Edgar
Fifth ditto, silver snuff box . . Matthew Mcin
Sixth ditto, gold chain . . W. Dixon
Seventh ditto, gold chain . . Jos. Dixon
Eighth ditto, gold chain . . J Wright

11 STONE PRIZE—ALL COMERS.

First prize, silver cup and £10 . J. Milburn
Second ditto, £6 . . . . James Edgar
Third ditto, £4 . . . . Jos. Allison
Fourth ditto, £2 . . . . James Scott
Fifth ditto, £2 . . . . John Snowdon
Sixth ditto, £2 . . . . John Graham
Seventh ditto, £1 . . . J. Collins
Eighth ditto, £1 . . . G. Sanderson
Ninth ditto, £1 . . . . J. Harrison
Tenth ditto, £1 . . . . Walter Armstrong
Eleventh ditto, £1 . . . J. Wright
Twelfth ditto, £1 . . . R. Moffatt

Hurdle Race.

First prize, £3 10s. . . . R. Musgrove
Second ditto, £1 10s. . . . J. Williams
Third ditto, 10s. . . . . Archibald Bell

Pole Leaping.

Tie for } £4 { . . R. Musgrove
First and Second } { . . J. Allison
Third ditto, £1 15s. . . . James Baines
Fourth ditto, 15s. . . . William Rake

N

ALL WEIGHTS—ALL COMERS.

First prize, silver cup and £14 . William Jameson
Second ditto, £8 . . . . William Armstrong
Third ditto, £4 . . . . John Snowdon
Fourth ditto, £4 . . . . Jos. Allison
Fifth ditto, £2 10s. . . . W. Timperton
Sixth ditto, £2 10s. . . . Richard Wright
Seventh ditto, £2 10s. . . . J. Collins
Eighth ditto, £1 . . . . J. Edgar
Ninth ditto, £1 . . . . S. King
Tenth ditto, £1 . . . . J. Allison
Eleventh ditto, £1 . . . Walter Armstrong
Twelfth ditto, £1 . . . R. Tomlinson
Thirteenth ditto, £1 . . . Jos. Dixon
Fourteenth ditto, £1 . . . T. Moffatt

Neatest Costume.

Matthew Mein,
Richard Wright, } each 10s. 6d.

1868.

The Annual General Meeting of the Society was held at the " Salutation Hotel," Newgate Street, on Feb. 19th, when the following officers were elected :—

CHAIRMAN.
Mr. William Leggett.

VICE-CHAIRMAN.
Major Wills.

TREASURER.
Mr. Alex. Scott.

HON. SEC.
Mr. R. Margetson (resigned).

Mr. Walter Armstrong was elected Hon. Sec. on the 11th of March.

STEWARDS.
Mr. Jos. Dixon, Bow
„ Joseph Dixon
„ William Topping
„ Gavin Irving
„ D. Wilson
„ E. Stainton
„ C. Atkins

At a subsequent meeting, the Chairman having announced that Mr. Margetson had resigned the office of Secretary, Mr. Walter Armstrong was elected to fill the vacant position. Messrs. William Thomas Thwaites, J. C. Thwaites, and Mr. John Sawer, were also elected as Stewards.

GOOD FRIDAY AT THE AGRICULTURAL HALL.

The great annual gathering took place at the Agricultural Hall on Good Friday, April 10th. The programme contained the names of the most cele-brated wrestlers from the North. There was also a large entry for the London Prize, which included the silver cup given by Mr. Charles Rudkin. A prize was this year offered for $9\frac{1}{2}$ stone men, who, by the way, generally show more science than their heavier brethren. This is a class of wrestlers which certainly ought to be encouraged. A great many young men coming from the North do not scale more than this weight, consequently they are deterred from wrestling, because they would have no chance in the 11 stone prize. Naturally they are discouraged, and soon lose all interest in the sport. The best amateurs we have had of late years have been $9\frac{1}{2}$ stone men, and although they have won prizes in the 11 stone class, it has been against fearful odds. If the $9\frac{1}{2}$ stone prize is a success in the country, where bone and sinew are more extensively de-

veloped, surely, here in London, amongst men whose
sedentary habits tend to reduce their weight so considerably, a feather weight prize ought to produce
the largest entry.

The all weight prize was very interesting, but
which, as a matter of course, resolved itself into a
match between Wright and Jameson. The spectators seemed much delighted with the pole-leaping,
which was keenly contested. The very judicious
prize, given for the neatest costume, produced a good
effect, and the contrast between the elegant tights,
and the "breeks and black stockings" of former
days was very great. There was an immense attendance, almost the largest ever known. The telegraph
boards, showing each competitors' number corre-
sponding with his name on the programme, was a well-
conceived idea, and carried out to perfection, under
the active superintendence of Mr. Samuel Cochrane.
Altogether the meeting was a very successful one,
the proceeds enabling the Committee to resume their
very laudable practice of subscribing to the benevolent institutions of the two counties. Umpires,
Messrs. Mein and Wills. Referee, Mr. Leggett.

The sports opened with the

9½ STONE MEN—ALL COMERS.

Second Round.

Stood.	Fell.
Jas. Furness	John Carter
John Tiffin	H. Chapman

Stood.	Fell.
T. Waugh	W. Armstrong
G. Graham	R. Routledge
J. Tomlinson	J. Gilliburn
John Graham	W. Park
Jos. Scaife	W. Stevens

G. Sanderson, odd man

Third Round.

G. Sanderson	T. Waugh
John Graham	J. Tomlinson
George Graham	Jos. Scaife
J. Tiffin	J. Moncrief
J. Furness	J. Walsh

Sanderson hiped Waugh, Graham cross-buttocked Tomlinson. The most exciting struggle of the round was between Tiffin and Moncrief; they were an endless time in getting hold, each trying to gain an advantage. Tiffin, as a matter of course, got the better hold, and, working his man round, threw him with a cross-buttock.

Fourth Round.

Stood.	Fell.
G. Sanderson	J. Furness
J. Tiffin	George Graham

John Graham, odd man

Sanderson hiped Furness easily. George Graham was too young for Tiffin, who turned in and buttocked him.

Fifth Round.

Stood.	Fell.
J. Tiffin	John Graham

G. Sanderson, odd man

Immense excitement prevailed when it transpired that Tiffin and John Graham were drawn together.

Tiffin struggled hard for a superior hold but all in vain, and was, for once, obliged to be content with a fair grip. He immediately made tracks for a buttock. Graham, however, happened to be looking out for that particular chip, and stopped the manœuvre, when the "old un," as quick as lightning, tried the outside stroke, which Graham resisted on the first attempt, but, failing the second, was thrown.

Final Falls.

Stood.	Fell.
George Sanderson	J. Tiffin
George Sanderson	J. Tiffin

The great reputation of Tiffin, the acknowledged champion of the "feather weights," rendered him the favourite when the two men stood up for the final falls. The London men, however, had great confidence in their old friend, George Sanderson, and a hearty cheer greeted him as he shook hands with the "invincible" before taking the first hold. Tiffin was the first to show play with the outside stroke, which was completely thrown away upon his opponent, for Sanderson gathered him up in his arms, and hiped him beautifully. The delight of the audience knew no bounds when Sanderson threw the little champion, and cries of " Bravo, Geordie," were heard all round the hall. After a pause, they came together again, but the struggle was of short duration. Tiffin failed to click his man, his friends calling out " Buttock him, Tiffin." Sanderson immediately took the hint, and floored his man with a splendid cross-buttock. The spectators were much delighted at the victory of Sanderson, who almost more than any other wrestler, deserves the popularity he enjoys. After the excitement was a little allayed, his friends gathered anxiously round him, and after many congratulations had been passed, some one said, " How did you fell him, Geordie ?" " Why, man," said George, " I crossed him baith legs, and fairly buried hin."

The hurdle race was won by J. Williams ; J. Walsh second.

All Weights—All Comers.

Second Round.

Stood.	Fell.
R. Wright	J. Thompson
J. Allison	J. Sproat
John Graham	J. Williams
E. Dobson	W. Holliday
C. Kennedy	R. Bowman
J. Tiffin	J. Tomlinson
T. Walker	J. Hilton
R. Tomlinson	T. Stevens
Wm. Park	H. Chapman
R. Coulthard	J. Furness
Jas. Edgar	M. Mein
G. Steadman	T. Cowing
W. Jameson	W. Stevens
J. Bell	T. Moffatt
W. Lawson	James Scott

Scott was not in anything like his usual trim, and was rather easily hiped by Lawson.

Third Round.

Stood.	Fell.
J. Tiffin	J. Thompson
C. Kennedy	E. Dobson
J. Bell	R. Tomlinson
R. Wright	J. Wright
W. Lawson	R. Coulthard
Wm. Park	G. Steadman
W. Jameson	J. Allison
J. Edgar	T. Walker

John Graham, Longtown, odd man

Tiffin buttocked Thompson cleverly, after a very exciting struggle. Dick Wright playfully threw J. Wright, throwing a semi-somersault over his remains. Lawson met a good match in R. Coulthard; more than once the Jarrow champion was within an ace of being thrown, but at length he improved his hold, and threw Coulthard with the hipe in a most superb manner. W. Park electrified the spectators by throwing Geo. Steadman, a man nearly twice his own weight.

Fourth Round.

Stood.	Fell.
C. Kennedy	J. Graham, Longtown
Wm. Jameson	W. Park
R. Wright	J. Tiffin
J. Edgar	J. Bell

W. Lawson, odd man.

Jameson, the biggest man at present wrestling was drawn against the smallest man of the light weights, W. Park, of Cockermouth. The contrast between the two can be imagined: Jameson being about 16 stone, and Park under $9\frac{1}{2}$ stone. Tiffin, who was in the ring at the same time, being drawn against Wright, suggested that he ought to be allowed to assist Park, when the champion playfully opened, his arms to receive them both. In the actual wrestle, Jameson lifted Park and laid him down like a pound-weight. Wright threw Tiffin quite as easily.

Fifth Round.

Stood.	Fell.
R. Wright	C. Kennedy
W. Jameson	W. Lawson

J. Edgar, odd man

In this round, Wright and Jameson threw their two opponents without an effort.

Sixth Round.

Stood.	Fell.
William Jameson	J. Edgar

R. Wright, odd man

Final Falls.

R. Wright	W. Jameson
R. Wright	W. Jameson

The champions soon got hold, and after a little dodging, slipped. At once they got into grips again, both seeming anxious to make play. Jameson tried to lift Wright, but Dick preferred keeping on the ground, and watching his opportunity, threw his opponent with the outside stoke. The result was greeted with loud cheering. An interval of five minutes, and the rivals met for the second fall. This time Dick availed himself of his celebrated chip and twisted Jameson from off his breast. The cheering was tremendous, and Wright was carried round the ring in triumph.

Pole Leaping.

J. Allison, of Kendal, won the first prize for the

pole leaping, clearing 10 feet 3 inches. James Baines was second. Allison was a troublesome customer to Musgrove last year, and divided the prize with him.

The London Prize.

MEN NOT EXCEEDING 11 STONE.

Second Round.

Stood.	Fell.
Matthew Mein	T. Stevens
J. Donald	J. Walsh
J. Gilliburn	R. Atkinson
G. Sanderson	J. Williams
John Graham	H. Chapman
Tom Cowing	J. Graham, Longtown
Jos. Dixon	James Furness
J. Edgar	J. Thompson
T. Waugh	R. Bewley
R. Coulthard	W. Stevens

Third Round.

J. Edgar	J. Donald
G. Sanderson	J. Williams
Tom Cowing	T. Waugh
R. Coulthard	J. Tomlinson
M. Mein	J. Gilliburn
John Graham	Jos. Dixon

A smart wrestle between John Graham and Jos. Dixon, resulting in what to some appeared to be a dog-fall, was given in by the Umpires in favour of Graham. The decision, though a just one, was much cavilled at, and gave rise to a very animated discussion.

Fourth Round.

Stood.	Fell.
J. Edgar	G. Sanderson
Tom Cowing	M. Mein
R. Coulthard	John Graham

Fifth Round.

Stood.	Fell.
J. Edgar	Tom Cowing

R. Coulthard, odd man

Final Falls.

R. Coulthard	J. Edgar
J. Edgar	R. Coulthard
R. Coulthard	J. Edgar

G. Sanderson wrestled well for this prize considering that he was suffering from a sprained instep. Old Robert Atkinson too struggled gamely, but his old fashioned chip, viz., the back heel is not good enough for the young blood he has to meet every year. Very few prizes have fallen to the old man's share during the many years he has been a competitor on Good Friday; yet, notwithstanding the fact that he is not particularly celebrated for his skill in the art of wrestling, his appearance is always the signal for a round of cheering, and a Good Friday would scarcely be considered complete without his venerable head and " breeks and grey stockings."

The final falls between Coulthard and Edgar were very interesting displays of science, and were well contested. Coulthard gained the first fall by the hank. In the second trial Edgar threw his opponent with the swinging hipe. They had now each gained a fall, and the last bout created much interest, Coulthard finally throwing Edgar by the inside click, thus winning the London prize.

The prizes were awarded as below :—

9½-STONE PRIZE—ALL COMERS.

First prize, a silver cup	.	.	G. Sanderson
Second ditto, £4 0 0	.	.	Jos. Tiffin
Third ditto, 2 10 0	.	.	John Graham
Fourth ditto, 1 10 0	.	.	George Graham
Fifth ditto, 0 15 0	.	.	J. Furness
Sixth ditto, 0 15 0	.	.	J. Walsh
Seventh ditto, 0 15 0	.	.	J. Moncrief
Eighth ditto, 0 15 0	.	.	J. Scaife
Ninth ditto, 0 15 0	.	.	J. Tomlinson
Tenth ditto, 0 15 0	.	.	T. Waugh

Pole Leaping.

First prize, £3 0 0	.	.	J. Allison
Second ditto, 2 0 0	.	.	J. Baines
Third ditto, 1 0 0	.	.	John Graham

Neatest Costume.

First prize, £1 10 0	.	.	Matthew Mein

ALL WEIGHTS—ALL COMERS.

First prize, £10 0 0	R. Wright
Second ditto, 6 0 0	William Jameson
Third ditto, 4 0 0	James Edgar
Fourth ditto, 3 0 0	William Lawson
Fifth ditto, 3 0 0	C. Kennedy
Sixth ditto, 2 0 0	J. Bell
Seventh ditto, 2 0 0	J. Tiffin
Eighth ditto, 2 0 0	William Park
Ninth ditto, 2 0 0	John Graham, Longtown

Hurdle Race.

First prize, £3 0 0	J. Williams
Second ditto, 2 0 0	J. Walsh

The London Prize.

First prize, silver cup	.	. R. Coulthard
Second ditto, silver watch	.	James Edgar

Third ditto, silver snuff box	.	Tom Cowing
Fourth ditto, silver snuff box		John Graham
Fifth ditto, gold Albert	.	Matthew Mein
Sixth ditto, gold Albert .	.	G. Sanderson
Seventh ditto, gold Albert	.	Jos. Dixon
Eighth ditto, gold Albert	.	J. Gilliburn

The annual dinner took place at the "Salutation Hotel," Newgate-street, on Wednesday, the 13th of May. Mr. Leggett occupied the chair, supported by Messrs. Thomas Mein, Walter Armstrong (Hon. Sec.), S. Cochrane, William Routledge, Matthew Mein, Geo. Sanderson, William Topping, William Thwaites, J. C. Thwaites, Gavin Irving, Jos. Dixon, &c. After the usual loyal and patriotic toasts had been duly honoured, the Chairman gave the toast of the evening, "Success to the Cumberland and Westmoreland Wrestling Society." The healths of the Chairman, Vice-Chairman. Hon. Secretary, and Treasurer having been proposed and responded to, the Chairman, in a few well-chosen words, gave the ever popular toast of "The Bonnie Lassies of Cumberland and Westmoreland," calling upon Mr. William Topping to respond. Mr. Topping replied in a very graceful and humorous speech, disclaiming, however, any pretensions to being the fittest person to do honour to such a toast. The remainder of the evening was enlivened by some excellent singing, and a very satisfactory year was brought to a close.

1869.

The Annual General Meeting was held at the " Salutation Hotel," Newgate-street, on Wednesday the 26th January, when a large number of influential members of the Society were present. The balance sheet, showing a surplus of over £40, after giving a donation of twenty guineas to the benevolent institutions connected with the two counties, having been read by the Secretary and unanimously adopted by the meeting, the following gentlemen were elected as Stewards for the year.

CHAIRMAN.　　　　　TREASURER.

Mr. William Leggett　　Mr. Thomas Mein

HON. SECRETARY.

Mr. Walter Armstrong

STEWARDS.

Mr. C. Atkins
„ William Atkinson
„ Jos. Dixon
„ G. Irving
„ J. C. Thwaites
„ William Topping
„ J. Illingworth
„ S. Hewetson
„ T. Moffatt
„ E. Stainton
„ William T. Thwaites
„ P. Twentyman

The proceedings were of a very satisfactory character, the members expressing themselves highly pleased with the exertions of the Committee during the previous year.

Great efforts were made to render the anniversary on Good Friday a successful one. A public meeting was held every week up to the day, and frequently a private Committee meeting in addition. A number of men carrying sandwich boards with large placards of the sports, were sent round the principal thoroughfares in the metropolis, who at the same time distributed 20,000 of the following handbills :—

"CUMBERLAND AND WESTMORELAND WRESTLING SOCIETY.

"The great Annual Meeting of the above Society will take place at the Agricultural Hall, Islington, on Good Friday, March 26th 1869.

"This will be the sixth successive year in which these popular sports have been held at the same place, and, to judge from the increase in the number of spectators each year, the public interest has not abated, neither has there been any falling off in the wrestling, nor in the manner of carrying out the attractive Programmes issued year after year. One of the objects of this Society is to assist in supporting two benevolent institutions, although the origin of the Association was to afford an opportunity for the natives of the two great wrestling counties of Cum-

berland and Westmoreland to meet once a year for
the purpose of engaging in those exercises for which
they have obtained a world-wide celebrity.

"The list of prizes this year is divided into three
classes, viz. :—London residents not exceeding eleven
stones, all comers from the North not exceeding
eleven stones, and the great champion prize for men
of all weights. Prizes also for hurdle racing and
pole leaping will be offered sufficient to induce the
best men from the North to put in an appearance.

"The celebrated wrestlers, Richard Wright of
Longtown, and William Jameson, of Penrith, have both
been specially invited on this occasion. It may be
interesting to the public to say a few words respect-
ing these two mighty exponents of the art of wrestling. Richard Wright, or as he is popularly styled,
the "Border Champion," weighs about 14 stones,
and is by far the most scientific wrestler the present
generation has seen. The dexterity of his movements
is something marvellous, and the clever manner in
which he disposes of a burly antagonist, scarcely less
formidable looking than himself, must be seen at the
Agricultural Hall, on Good Friday, to be thoroughly
appreciated. During the last fifteen years he has
won over 500 prizes, and there is not a ring in
England from which he has not taken either a cup or
a belt. William Jameson commenced his career as a
pole leaper, being then a mere stripling ; his increas-

ing weight, however, soon reminded him that his attention must be turned to something different, and wrestling became his chief pursuit. He is now about 16 stones in weight, and, although he does not follow pole leaping as a profession, he occasionally competes for a prize, and can even yet clear the cross-bar at an altitude of ten feet, a feat unparalleled in athletic history, when his great size is taken into consideration. The burly form of the great *athlète* as he clears the cross-bar, his enormous bulk high in the air, making the pole quiver under his tremendous weight, is more like a fable than a reality.

"The lithe Musgrove will also be there, the representative of a race of pole leapers; younger brother of the late champion, who cleared 11 feet 6 inches.

"A new feature will be introduced into the steeplechase in the shape of a water jump, which is expected to create much amusement.

"The pole leaping and steeplechase will come off last, to enable those visitors arriving late, to witness this interesting portion of the day's sports.

"The Committee have great pleasure in informing the public that no pains have been spared to render the anniversary on Good Friday worthy the high position of the Society, and that arrangements have been made to secure every comfort to all classes of spectators. The Gates will open at One, p.m. Admission, 1s. ; Front seats, 2s. 6d. ; Reserved seats, 5s.

"WALTER ARMSTRONG, *Hon. Sec.*"

The wrestling was again held at the Agricultural Hall. The great and increasing popularity of the sports attracted an immense gathering. Every part of the capacious building was crowded with well-dressed men, presenting a perfect sea of faces. As usual, the quiet decorum of the spectators was remarkable; not the semblance of chaff was heard either at the officials or competitors, which must have surprised most strangers who have been accustomed to see mixed assemblages of a similar kind. The cockney appeared quite out of his element amidst the peculiar dialect which everywhere assailed him, and frequently displayed the utmost astonishment at the conversation going on around him, more especially at some of the technical terms used by the wrestlers. The uninitiated spectator would also be surprised sometimes to see a wrestler standing on his head, and seemingly in a terrible plight, when he would be pulled up by the hand, give himself a shake together, and be ready for the fray again.

The proceedings commenced a little before two o'clock with the prize for London men, which was won by John Thompson, Penrith; the celebrated John Graham taking second honours. Graham wrestled very gamely, but was evidently not in his best "fettle." The spectators were much pleased at Thompson's victory, and cheered him to the echo. J. Beeby won the hurdle race very easily from Musgrove, whose "performance" gave anything but satisfaction,—a circumstance which is much to be regretted, and if allowed to be repeated will have a very unfavourable effect on the sports, which have always been carried out, on the part of the competitors, with the strictest integrity. The Society cannot be too severe in dealing with such unworthy attempts at imposition. Independent of this drawback, the amusement caused by the water jump in the race was of a most sensational kind; several of the competitors jumped fairly into the pool, and as many as three were in at the same time, Tom Robinson actually sitting down in it, convulsing the spectators with laughter. The display of pole-leaping was the best ever seen at the Hall, Musgrove exceeded all his previous efforts, closely followed, however, by a new aspirant, viz.:—D. Anderson, of Alnwick. The greatest sensation, however, was caused in the heavy weight prize, by the celebrated Border champion, Richard Wright, falling in the first round to an amateur of the name of Picton. It was a great fluke, and perfectly petrified the spectators, as it is well known that no two men in the world can throw the scientific Dick. Jameson made short work of the vanquisher of Wright in the following round, but fell himself in the fourth round, when buttocking Lawson. The overthrow of Jameson and Wright was quite unexpected.

The arrangements gave universal satisfaction. The *Daily Telegraph* commenting upon the proceedings remarks :—" The present celebration was marked by business-like activity on the part of the Committee and officers, and was in all essential respects highly creditable to the Society."

The Umpires were Messrs. William Thos. Thwaites and Major Wills. Referee, Mr. R. Margetson.

THE LONDON PRIZE—MEN NOT EXCEEDING 11 STONE.

Second Round.

Stood.	Fell.
T. Cowing	R. Watson
T. Moore	T. Jackson
H. Johnston	J. G. Thompson
J. Furness	D. Johnstone
R. Coulthard	T. Price
J. Thompson	G. Sanderson
John Graham (Carlisle)	G. W. Wood
T. Moffatt	J. Parkin
J. Wilson	R. Moffatt
Matthew Mein	R. Tomlinson
J. Reed	J. Baty
J. Graham (Longtown)	W. Armstrong
J. Mitchell	W. Little
J. Donald	J. G. Thompson

H. Atkinson, odd man.

This round was opened by Cowing and Watson, the latter of whom was easily thrown by the half-buttock. Coulthard threw Price with the swinging hipe. Sanderson and Thompson had a tough bout; Sanderson inserted the inside click but had not strength enough to bear his man down, and Thompson fairly wore him out.

Third Round.

Stood.	Fell.
J. Graham (Carlisle)	T. Moore
T. Cowing	J. Graham (Longtown)
J. Thompson	J. Wilson
R. Coulthard	H. Johnstone
T. Moffatt	J. Reed
M. Mein	J. Donald
J. Mitchell	H. Atkinson
J. Tomlinson	J. Furness

T. Walker, odd man.

Graham of Longtown and Cowing had an exciting struggle, the latter finally throwing his man with the hipe. Thompson threw Wilson with the buttock, and Coulthard threw Johnston with the swinging hipe.

Fourth Round.

Stood.	Fell.
J. Thompson	T. Moffatt
J. Graham (Carlisle)	J. Mitchell
R. Coulthard	T. Walker
M. Mein	J. Cowing

J. Tomlinson, odd man.

Thompson and Moffatt were a long time in the ring, the first hold resulting in a slip; when they came together again, Thompson grassed his man in a very smart manner. Matthew Mein hanked Tom Cowing.

Fifth Round.

Stood.	Fell.
J. Graham (Carlisle)	J. Tomlinson
J. Thompson	R. Coulthard

M. Mein, odd man

Graham threw Tomlinson with a good cross-buttock. Thompson swung Coulthard fairly on to his back.

Fourth Round.

Stood.	Fell.
J. Thompson	M. Mein
J. Graham, odd man	

Final Falls.

Stood.	Fell.
J. Thompson	J. Graham
J. Graham	J. Thompson
J. Thompson	J. Graham

No sooner had they got hold when Thompson threw Graham with the swing. In the second struggle Graham took hold quickly and threw his man with a scientific inside click for which he is famous; in the last hold Graham was compelled to succumb to superior weight and strength.

Hurdle Race.

J. Beeby	.	.	.	First
R. Musgrove		.	.	Second
J. Williams		.	.	Third
D. Anderson		.	.	Fourth

11 STONE PRIZE—ALL COMERS.

Third Round.

Stood.	Fell.
J. Milburn	R. Musgrove
J. Donald	M. Mein
W. Lawson	J. Tomlinson
J. Allison	R. Coulthard
T. Cowing	R. Atkinson
C. Kennedy	W. Beattie
D. Wills	T. Moffatt

Lawson threw Tomlinson with a beautiful hipe. Coulthard "laid" down to Jos. Allison. The veteran,

R. Atkinson, got the back heel in with Cowing, but he was unable to make use of it, as his antagonist by sheer strength bored him down, the old man making a good struggle of it to the last.

Fourth Round.

Stood.	Fell.
J. Milburn	D. Wills
J. Allison	J. Donald
W. Lawson	T. Cowing
C. Kennedy	T. Walker

Fifth Round.

W. Lawson	J. Allison
C. Kennedy	J. Milburn

An exciting contest took place between Lawson and Allison. The latter is the stouter built man, but Lawson is the prettier wrestler. Each tried all he knew. Lawson eventually disposed of his man with the hipe. Kennedy threw Milburn very cleverly with the inside click.

Final Falls.

Stood.	Fell.
W. Lawson	C. Kennedy
C. Kennedy	W. Lawson
W. Lawson	C. Kennedy

The final falls were of very short duration. Kennedy fell to the buttock in the first trial, in the second he managed to throw Lawson by slipping his head; Lawson, however, finally buttocked Kennedy high in the air, and was proclaimed the winner.

The overthrow of Rich. Wright in the first round, as before stated, was a surprise to every one. He was drawn against A. Picton, an amateur, and quite unknown to fame. They were just about the same height, and not much difference in their weight; perhaps Picton might be a little the heavier. Several times they essayed to get hold. Wright's friends were very impatient at his wasting so much time on a mere novice, calling out to him, " Dad him doon, Dick." Wright, perhaps, a little nettled, took hold at the wrong time, made a sudden move, missed his foot, and fell. There was no mistake about it, although difficult to realize at the time. The greatest excitement ensued, and the cheering was tremendous as Picton carried his ticket to the reporter's table. This unexpected incident altered the aspect of affairs, and, to all appearance, left Jameson master of the field. The result, however, proved otherwise, much to the delight of the spectators, who seemed to think that Jameson and Wright had won the first prize quite often enough.

ALL WEIGHTS—ALL COMERS.
Third Round.

Stood.	Fell.
R. Mason	R. Briscoe
J. Holmes	R. Musgrove
G. Steadman	J. Allison
G. Sanderson	T. Moffatt
J. Graham	T. Walker

Stood.	Fell.
W. Jameson	A. Picton
C. Kennedy	R. Coulthard

W. Lawson, odd man

Jameson and Picton soon got hold. The champion lifted Picton at once, and hiped him very carefully, sticking to him till they reached the ground, which they did, with a thud that resounded all over the ring.

Fourth Round.

Stood.	Fell.
W. Lawson	W. Jameson
R. Mason	T. Cowing
G. Steadman	J. Wright
C. Kennedy	J. Holmes
G. Sanderson	J. Graham

The issue between Lawson and Jameson was unlooked for. It looked almost ridiculous for Lawson to strike the huge leg of Jameson (which seemed immovable), from the ground. In attempting to buttock Lawson, Jameson slipped, and fell under him. The greatest excitement prevailed; a great number of the spectators maintained it was a dog-fall. However, the referee decided that Jameson had been thrown, but it took some time to convince the people that the champion was really down.

Fifth Round.

Stood.	Fell.
W. Lawson	C. Kennedy
G. Steadman	R. Mason

George Sanderson, odd man

Sixth Round.

Stood.	Fell.
W. Lawson	G. Sanderson

G. Steadman, odd man

W. Lawson had a hard struggle to get rid of Sanderson. Lawson hiped his man, thinking he had nothing to do but drop him to ground, instead of which Sanderson landed on his feet, when his opponent again applied the hipe successfully.

Final Falls.

Stood.	Fell.
G. Steadman	W. Lawson
W. Lawson	G. Steadman
G. Steadman	W. Lawson

The men, as they stood up for the final falls, were loudly cheered. Both are splendid wrestlers. Lawson, the most scientific of the two, laboured under the disadvantage of being at least two stone lighter than his opponent, who is also a much younger man, and bids fair to be a formidable rival to Wright and Jameson. In the first bout Lawson tried the buttock, but failed, Steadman screwing him down over his knee. On getting hold again Lawson gained the fall by a smart buttock. The time occupied in wrestling the final falls was twenty minutes; the men slipped hold no fewer than four times. Lawson by this time was gradually tiring, and, when they got into grips, Steadman, the fresher of the two, bored his man down. The men were well matched, and a finer struggle has seldom been witnessed. The cheers' which were loud and long, were equally and deservedly bestowed on both men.

Pole Leaping.

For this event there were a dozen entries, but only eight came to the scratch, namely, Mark Shearman, of Keswick; J. Beeby, Little Orton; John Graham, Carlisle; R. Musgrove, Cockermouth; D. Anderson, Alnwick; William Jameson, Penrith; James Baines, Penrith; J. Tomlinson, Carlisle. The standard was first hoisted at 6 feet 6 inches, but before the height became 8 feet 6 inches, Beeby, Graham, Tomlinson, and William Jameson, retired—the latter, considering that he scaled over 16 stone, jumped with remarkable agility. Shearman and Baines also retired at 9 feet 6 inches, at which height they tied. The issue was now left to Musgrove and Anderson. The latter made a gallant struggle against the now acknowledged champion with the pole. It was only when the bar was raised to 10 feet 7 inches that he retired, defeated, it is true, but not disgraced, as was testified by the applause which he carried with him out of the arena.

The sports were brought to a close at 8 o'clock, after which the prizes were awarded to the winners, as follows :—

ALL WEIGHTS.

First prize, £13 . . G. Steadman
Second ditto, £6 10s. . W. Lawson
Third ditto, £4 . . George Sanderson
Fourth ditto, £2 10s. . R. Mason
Fifth ditto, £2 10s. . C. Kennedy
Sixth ditto, £1 10s. . John Graham
Seventh ditto, £1 10s. . J. Holmes
Eighth ditto, £1 10s. . J. Wright
Ninth ditto, £1 10s. . T. Cowing
Tenth ditto, £1 10s. . . William Jameson

11 STONE MEN—ALL COMERS.

First prize, £10 . . William Lawson
Second ditto, £5 . . C. Kennedy
Third ditto, £3 10s. . . J. Milburn
Fourth ditto, £3 10s. . Jos. Allison
Fifth ditto, £2 . . T. Walker
Sixth ditto, £2 . . T. Cowing
Seventh ditto, £2 . . J. Donald
Eighth ditto, £2 . . D. Wills

The London Prize.

	£	s.	d.	
First prize, a silver cup, value £10	10	0	} John Thompson
Cash	5	0	0	
Second ditto, silver watch .	7	0	0	John Graham
Third ditto, gold guard .	3	15	0	Matthew Mein
Fourth ditto, gold guard .	3	12	6	R. Coulthard
Fifth ditto, gold guard .	2	12	6	J. Tomlinson
Sixth ditto, gold guard .	2	12	6	T. Cowing
Seventh ditto, gold guard .	2	12	6	T. Walker
Eighth ditto, gold guard .	2	12	6	J. Mitchell

Pole Leaping.

	£	s.	d.	
First prize .	£3	10	0	R. Musgrove
Second ditto .	2	0	0	D. Anderson
Third ditto .	0	15	0	M. Sharman and J. Baines

Steeplechase.

First prize	.	.	£3 0 0	J. Beeby
Second ditto	.	.	1 10 0	R. Musgrove
Fourth ditto	.	.	0 10 0	J. Williams

Neatest Costume.

First prize	.	.	£1 10 0	Matthew Mein
Second ditto	.	.	0 10 0	Tom Moffatt

ANNUAL DINNER.

The Annual Dinner of the Society was held at the "Salutation Hotel," Newgate-street, on Wednesday' the 5th of May, Mr. Wm. Leggett in the chair, Major Wells occupied the Vice, supported by Messrs. Thos. Mein (Treasurer), Walter Armstrong (Hon. Sec.), R. Margetson, James Hodgson, Wm. Armstrong, Saml. Cochrane, George Felton, Wm. Topping, M. Mein, G. Irving, J. Dixon, Wm. Thos. Thwaites, Wm. Routledge, J. Illingworth, &c. After the usual loyal toasts had been duly honoured, the Chairman gave the Army, Navy, and Volunteers. Major Wills briefly responded for the former branch of the service, and Captain Margetson, of the (4th City R.V.C.) for the volunteers. He always felt great pleasure in responding on their behalf, and he could fully endorse the observation of the gallant Major, for in his younger days he (Captain Margetson) had also served in the army. He felt certain that the volunteer movement had been the great means of preserving peace, for their enemies would not dare to show their teeth while Great Britain had such an army of citizens as they now possessed. In the north, more particularly in their native counties, the movement had increased, and the inspecting generals had held them up as a pattern to others.

The Chairman next proposed the toast of the evening " Success to the Cumberland and Westmoreland Wrestling Society ;" and in doing so, remarked that the robust and healthy frames of those he saw before him, was a convincing proof, if any were wanting, that the art of wrestling was conducive to the well-being of its votaries, and rendered them better able to withstand the trials and anxieties to which men who are engaged in commercial pursuits are constantly exposed.

Capt. Margetson proposed the health of the Chairman.

The Chairman, in reply, said he had always endeavoured to make himself an independent member of the Society ; he had sided with no party, and should always continue to act in that spirit of neutrality which became a man who was placed in the position he had been.

Mr. Walter Armstrong, the Hon. Sec., then rose and said that " the Committee thought it would only be dealing fairly and courteously with the subscribers and supporters of the institution, to take the earliest opportunity of stating our financial position. We commenced this year with a balance of £40 13s. Ten guineas we received from Messrs. Spiers and Pond, in the shape of a silver cup ; £325 was taken on Good Friday, and the cash for tickets and donations amounted to about £80, making a total of £445. On the other side we paid the large sum of £100 for the Agricultural Hall. The prizes cost £122 12s. 6d., and sundry other expenses, say £100. •Twenty guineas presented to the two benevolent institutions of Cumberland and Westmoreland ; total, £343, leaving the handsome balance of £102 in hard cash, the largest surplus, with the exception of 1863 and 1864, for a number of years. There can be no doubt, gentlemen, that our expenses have been heavy, but the end has justified the means. In these advertising days it is necessary to keep pace with the times. The penny-wise system will never raise this Society to the position which it is destined to hold, namely, the first athletic society in the kingdom; and I hope, gentlemen, the day is not far distant when this Association will, by having a benevolent fund of its own, meet in a more efficient manner the wants of those who have passed into the sere and yellow leaf.

Mr. Jas. Hodgson proposed the health of the Treasurer, and the rest of the officers, to which Mr. Mein responded. Some excellent singing then followed,

Mr. Cochrane's " Digging for Gould," playing a conspicuous part. The last song of the evening was " John Peel," from Mr. Matthew Mein, which found a response in the hearts of all the north countrymen present.

WINNERS OF THE WRESTLING SINCE 1824.

	First.	Second.	Third.	
1824	John Dobson	J. Richardson	Wm. Graham	
1824	George Byers	Ths. Richardson	Joseph Budd	
1825	John Beaty	Wm. Graham	Joseph Lambert	First time over
1825	William Dent	Wm. Metcalf	John Cowing	Second ,,
1826	Robert Hall	Joseph Dobson		
1827	Wm. Graham	John Ellwood	Robert Winter	First time over
1827	William Mars	Wm. Fawcett	Joseph Stamper	Second ,,
1828	Wm. Percival	Thos. Fawcett	Joseph Dobson	First ,,
1828	Phil. Thompson	Jno. Atkinson	Wm. Robinson	Second ,,
1829	Jos Dobson	Jos. Stamper	Joseph Wills	First ,,
1829	Tim. Dobson	John Ellwood	Joseph Slack	Second ,,
1830	John Dixon	Tim Dobson	Thos. Thwaites	First ,,
1830	Wm. Fawcett	Jno. Atkinson	Thomas Bird	Second ,,
1831	Jos. Stamper	Stphn. Fawcett	Edward Ewin	First ,,
1831	Jno. Carruthers	Thos. Irving	Phil. Thompson	Second ,,
1832	Chris. Gaddes	John Lamb	H. Mossop	First ,,
1832	Joseph Wills	Jno. Carruthers	Thos. Thwaites	Second ,,
1833	Jno. Carruthers	Jas. Armstrong	J. Robinson	First ,,
1833	Thos. Abrams	Joseph Wills	Thos. Broklebank	Second ,,
1834	John Robinson	Jos. Wills, jnr.	Stephen Fawcett	First ,,
1834	Thos. Abrams	Geo. Brunskill	Wm. Brunskill	Second ,,
1835	J. Westgarth	Thomas Hall	Edwd. Dawson	Lgt. wts. und. 11 st.
1835	Geo. Brunskill	Jos. Wills, jnr.	Jos. Wills, snr.	All weights
1936	Jos. Wills, jnr.	Jos. Wills, snr.	John Harvey	First time over
1836	J. Harvey	Robinson Ridley	Thomas Hall	Second ,,
1837	Jos. Wills, senr.	Richard Metcalf	J. Armstrong	Heavy weights
1837	E. Dawson	R. James	J. Pearson	Lgt. wts. und. 11 st.
1838	Thos. Abrams	William Earl	John Wren	All weights
1838	H. Thompson	R. Gill	R. Foster	Hy. wts. un. 12¼ st.
1838	R. Margetson	J. Armstrong	R. Farriday	Lgt. wts. un. 11 st.
1839	J. Haig	J. Wills, jnr.	T. Abrams	All weights ,
1839	R. Margetson	J. Carruthers	J. Dixon	Hy. wts. un. 12¼ st.
1839	J. Armstrong	J. Gregson	W. Nicholson	Lgt. wts. un. 11 st.
1840	Jas. Haig	G. Brunskill	W. Faulder	All weights

P

	First.	Second.	Third.	
1840	T. Abrams	T. Donow	J. Gregson	Hy. wts. un. 12½ st.
1840	T. Sandford	P. Clemetson	Wm. Brown	Lgt. wts. und. 11 st.
1841	Jno. Armstrong	Thos. Plaskett	Rd. Margetson	Lgt. wts. und 11 st.
1841	Geo. Brunskill	E. Lamb	Rd. Margetson	All weights
1842	Jos. Wills, jnr.	Geo. Brunskill	John Dixon	All weights
1842	Thos. Hudson	D. Harrison	J. Swain	Lgt. wts. und. 11 st.
1843	Mark Morley	J. Norman	Geo. Brunskill	All weights
1843	Geo. Donaldson	F. Bowman	J. Bell	Lgt. wts. und. 11 st.
1844	W. Miller	A. Nelson	Rd. Margetson	All weights
1844	W. Morton	J. Simmons	J. Sill	Lgt. wts. und. 11 st.
1845	G. Brunskill	Thos. Millar	E. Gregson	All weights.
1845	Jer. Pearson	Wm. Harrison	Thos. Earl	Lgt. wts. und. 11 st.
1846	C. Dobson	Jos. Wills, jnr.	Jas. Haigh	Light weights
1846	Jthu. Whitehead	Sam. Pearson	Jno. Thompson	Lgt. wts. und. 11 st.
1847	Thos. Longmire	A. Dawson	Jos. Hallewell	All weights
1847	Jos. Halliwell	Jer. Pearson	J. Chicken	Lgt. wts. und. 11 st.
1848	J. Banks	J. Robinson	Corpl. Dixon	All weights
1848	J. Whitehead	J. Halliwell	R. Gash	Lgt. wts. und. 11 st.
1848	W. Walker	T. Walker	J. Rose	Lgt. wts. und. 9 st.
1849	R. Atkinson	Jos. Harrington	Anthouy Dawson	All weights
1849	Jthn. Whitehead	James Wilson	Thomas Walker	Lgt wts. und. 11 st.
1849	Jno. Dixon, jnr.	Jas. Irvine	Thomas Walker	Lgt. wts. und. 9 st.
1850	G. Brunskill	Corporal Edgar	Isaac Robinson	All weights
1850	John Dixon	Thos. Matthews	George Kershaw	Lgt. wts. und. 11 st.
1850	Chris. Fawcett	J. Shepherd	Gerard Raws	Lgt. wts. und. 9st.
1851	John Dixon	Corpl. Jos. Dixon	Sergt. Chalmers	All weights
1851	George Irving	John Dixon	John Steel	Lgt. wts. und 11 st.
	[Coldstream Guards			
1852	John Dixon	Alex. Scott	Thos. Whitfield	All weights
1852	Alex. Scott	James Bishop	John Dixon	Lgt. wts. und. 11 st.
1852	J. Greenhow	J. Hind	T. Teasdale	All weights
1852	J. Moss	Alex. Scott	T. Teasdale	Eight last standers
1853	Thomas Todd	Geo. Brunskill	Harry Howe	All weights
1853	Ths. Williamson	Harry Howe	Matthew Palmer	Lgt. wts. und. 11st.
1854	Geo. Brunskill	Alex. Scott	Robt. Greenhow	All weights
1854	James Scott	Joseph Tiffin	Thos. Dickinson	Lgt. wts. und. 11st.
1855	N. Faulkner	W. Shepherd	Alex. Scott	All weights
1855	Alex. Scott	J. Moorhouse	Joseph Tiffin	Lgt. wts. und. 11st.
1856	Geo. Brunskill	John Smith	Thomas Wood	All weights
1856	Joseph Tiffin	Harry Howe	J. Moorhouse	Lgt. wts. und. 11st.
1857	John Smith	Jos. Thompson	J. Routledge	All weights
1857	Jos. Thompson	William Banks	John Thompson	Lgt. wts. und. 11st.

	First	Second	Third
1858	T. Hetherington	Jos. Wilkinson	Jos. Thompson	All weights
1858	Geo. Gibson	John Smith	Thos. Saunders	Lgt. wts. und. 11st.
1859	T. Hetherington	Geo. Sanderson	W. Sewell	All weights
1859	Geo. Mason	J. Mason	Geo. Sanderson	Lgt. wts. und. 11st
1860	John Smith	Thos. Robinson	Math. Robinson	All weights
1860	John Mason	G. Mason	Math. Robinson	Lgt. wts. und. 11st.
1861	Wm. Jameson	Noble Ewbank	Richd. Wright	All weights
1861	Ben Cooper	John Smith	Geo. Sanderson	Lgt. wts. und. 11st.
1861	John Dixon	Wm. Gilchrist	Thomas Mein	do. Lon. prize
1861	Noble Ewbank	T. Rawlinson	James Scott	16 picked men
1862	Wm. Jameson	Richard Wright	J. Brunskill	All weights
1862	James Scott	George Scott	Wltr. Armstrong	Lgt. wts. und. 11st
1862	John Smith	John Dixon	Geo. Sanderson	do. Lon. prize
1863	Wm. Jameson	John Dixon	Wltr. Armstrong	All weights (Whit-Monday)
1863	Richard Wright	Wm. Jameson	Thos. Blackett	All weights
1863	George Scott	W. Thornthwaite	James Scott	Lgt. wts. und. 11st.
1863	R. Wetherall	John Smith	R. Ritson	do. Lon. prize
1864	Geo. Maxwell	Matthew Lee	J. Emmerson	All weights
1864	W. Watson	Jos. Allison	R. Blair	Lgt. wts. und. 11st.
1864	Rchd. Coulthard	W. Pearson	R. Tyson	do. Lon. prize
1864	G. Sanderson	Wltr. Armstrong	R. Tyson	Lgt. wts. und. 9½st. (Cremorne)
1864	R. Coulthard	J. Thompson	T. Robinson	All wts (Cremorne)
1865	John Mitchell	John Natrass	Jas. Scott	All weights
1865	Jos. Allison	James Scott	Henry Ivison	Lgt. wts. und. 11st.
1865	James Edgar	Wltr. Armstrong	Geo. Hunton	do. Lon. prize
1865	Wm. Jameson	Jos. Whitehead	W. Graham	All wts. (Cremorne)
1865	Archibald Bell	John Thompson	S. Hewitson	Lgt. wts. do
1865	R. Coulthard	John Milburn	R. Carruthers	Lgt. wts. do.
1866	Richd. Wright	Wm. Jameson	J. Emmerson	All weights
1866	John Milburn	James Scott	Joseph Allison	Lgt. wts. und. 11st.
1866	John Graham	Wm. Armstrong	Thos. Sanders	do. Lon. prize
1866	John Graham	J. Briggs	G. Sanderson	Lgt. wts. und. 9½st.
1867	Wm. Jameson	Wm. Armstrong	J. Snowdon	All weights
1867	Jno. Milburn	Jas. Edgar	Jos. Allison	Lgt. wts. und. 11st.
1867	John Graham	John Thompson	Thos. Moffatt	Lgt. wts. Lon. prize
1868	Richd. Wright	Wm. Jameson	Jas. Edgar	All weights
1868	R. Coulthard	Jas. Edgar	Thomas Cowing	Lgt. wts. Lon. prize
1868	G. Sanderson	J. Tiffin	John Graham	Lgt. wts. und. 9½st.
1869	G. Steadman	Wm. Lawson	G. Sanderson	All weights
1869	Wm. Lawson	Clem. Kennedy	J. Milburn	Lgt. wts. und. 11st.
1869	Jno. Thompson	John Graham	Matthew Mein	Lgt. wts. Lon. prize

LIST OF DONATIONS

TO THE

Cumberland Benevolent Institution, and the Westmoreland Society's Schools.

To the Cumberland Benevolent Institution.

		£	s	d
1836	... ...	£10	10	0
1845	Per R. Beck, Esq.	10	10	0
1846	„ Geo. Eilbeck, Esq., John James, Esq.	21	0	0
1847	„ Geo. Eilbeck, Esq.	10	10	0
1856	„ James Brown, Esq.	10	10	0
1857	„ Thomas Charlton, Esq.	10	10	0
1858	„ Wm. Leggett, Esq.	10	10	0
1859	„ Jas. Ellison, Esq., Jas. Hodgson, Esq.	21	0	0
1860	„ F. Bell, Esq., Thos. Clemitson, Esq....	21	0	0
1862	„ Wm. Armstrong, Esq., C. Little, Esq.	21	0	0
1863	„ T. Charlton, Esq., J. Thompson ...	21	0	0
1864	„ J. Scott Brown, Esq., Jos. Richardson, Esq	21	0	0
1868	„ Jos. Wells, Esq.	10	10	0
1869	„ Wm. Topping, Esq.	10	10	0
		£210	0	0

To the Westmoreland Society's Schools.

		£	s	d
1836	... ...	10	10	0
1845	... ...	10	10	0
1846	... ...	21	0	0
1847	Per William Thompson, Esq.	10	10	0
1856	„ E. Stainton, Esq....	10	10	0
1857	„ G. Wharton, Esq.	10	10	0
1858	„ G. D. Lund, Esq.	10	10	0
1859	„ J. Thompson, Esq., Geo. Gibson, Esq.	21	0	0
1860	„ R. Margetson, Esq., John Richardson, Esq.	21	0	0
1862	„ John Smith, Esq., Thos. Charlton, Esq.	21	0	0
1863	„ R. Margetson, Esq., Geo. Gibson, Esq.	21	0	0
1864	„ J. Hodgson, Esq., R. Atkinson, Esq...	21	0	0
1868	„ Wm. T. Thwaites, Esq.	10	10	0
1869	„ John Illingworth, Esq.	10	10	0
		£210	0	0

Also iu the year 1864.

To COMMERCIAL TRAVELLERS' SCHOOLS.

Per Frank Bell, Esq. £10 10 0

To WAREHOUSEMEN AND CLERKS' SCHOOLS.

Per James Brown, Esq. £10 10 0

List of amounts given in prizes during the last thirteen years :—

Year	Place					£	s	d
1857,	at Hackney Wick	...	...	...	...	£35	5	0
1858,	ditto	...	...	...	...	35	15	0
1859,	ditto	...	...	...	...	30	14	0
1860,	Hornsey Wood House	...	...	...		53	10	0
1861,	ditto	...	...	...	...	93	5	0
1862,	ditto	...	...	...	...	93	8	0
1863,	ditto	...	...	...	...	102	4	0
1864,	Agricultural Hall	...	...	...	...	128	2	0
1865,	ditto	...	...	...	...	153	10	0
1865,	Cremorne Gardens	...	...	...	...	105	0	0
1866,	Agricultural Hall	...	...	...	...	137	14	6
1867,	ditto	...	...	...	...	145	11	6
1868,	ditto	...	...	...	...	103	6	0
1869,	ditto	...	...	...	...	122	12	6

RULES.

The following revised rules were passed at a general meeting held at the "Salutation Hotel," Newgate-street, on the 6th March, 1867.

1.—That this Society shall be designated the CUMBERLAND AND WESTMORELAND WRESTLING SOCIETY.

2.—That the benefits conferred by this Society shall be confined to Natives of Cumberland and Westmoreland, and at the discretion of the Committee to other North-country men, to whom suitable Prizes shall be given to be Wrestled for, on GOOD FRIDAY, in each year; the amount and number of such Prizes to be regulated by the Committee; and should any surplus money arise, over and above £150, that power shall be given to the Committee to decide the amount of Gift (if any), which shall be handed over to the Benevolent Institutions of Cumberland and Westmoreland; all such Gifts from this Society, be it understood, shall be equally divided betwixt the two.

3.—That the government of this Society shall be vested in a Committee of Eleven Members, consisting of Chairman, Vice-Chairman, Treasurer, Secretary, and seven Stewards, to be elected annually, by ballot or otherwise, that the Committee shall have full power, and that all its transactions shall be binding until the election of the new Committee, at the Annual General Meeting: and that Five of the Committee shall be a Quorum.

4.—That no person shall be eligible to be elected on the Committee, or become a Member of this Society, or be allowed to propose any Resolution, or Vote at any Meeting, who has not subscribed Two Shillings and Sixpence or upwards; or be allowed to Wrestle, unless his Subscription has been duly paid up before the time of Wrestling.

5.—That the Secretary shall read a Report of the Transactions of the Committee whenever the same shall be required.

6.—That any Member of the Society having a Complaint to make, shall make it to the Secretary, in writing, who shall have power, at all times, to call a Private Meeting of the Committee for the dispatch of such business, and their decision upon it shall be final.

7.—That all sums of money arising from Subscriptions or otherwise shall be paid into the hands of the Treasurer every Thursday or other night, when the Meetings take place, for the necessary expenses of the Society.

8.—That proper books shall be provided for the use of the Society, and all Receipts and Disbursements be entered therein, in such manner as the Committee shall direct.

9.—That at the General Meetings of the Committee (at which subscribers shall be allowed to attend) the Treasurer shall produce his accounts of Receipts and Payments, and Cash in hand, the particulars of which shall be entered as part of the Minutes.

10.—That the number and amount of Prizes, and the different Classes of Weights, shall be regulated by the Committee.

11.—That should any dispute arise in the Ring betwixt the Umpires, the decision of the Referee shall be final; and any individual refusing to conform to the usual Rules of Wrestling, either by refusing to take fair hold—to Wrestle over again or otherwise—the Umpire shall have full power to strike out his name.

12.—That should any Member or Members do any act to the dishonour or prejudice of the Society, either in the Ring or out of it, the Committee shall have full power to expel him or them from the Society; but that it shall not be considered a disgrace for any Member of the Society to challenge another to Wrestle, provided it is done privately, and not by public advertisement (with his knowledge and and consent); but if any Member shall challenge, or cause another to be challenged by public advertisement, the Committee shall expel him from the Society.

13.—That should any Member buy or sell, or offer to buy or sell, a Fall; or by neglecting to do his best, and thereby suffer himself to be unfairly thrown, he shall be expelled from the Society; and any Prize he may have been entitled to, shall be forfeited by him, and given to the next in rotation.

14.—That the Anniversary shall take place immediately after the Wrestling, when the Chairman shall deliver the Prizes to each successful Competitor.

15.—That a Private Meeting of the Committee and Stewards be convened, a fortnight after Good Friday, for the settlement of Accounts, that a General Meeting of the Society, may be held not later than midsummer, when a dinner shall be provided at Two Shillings and Sixpence, each Member. That Two Tickets shall be allowed to each Member of the Committee, at the Expense of the Society; and that the Tickets shall express the Time and Place of Meeting.

16.—That the Balance Sheet be Printed and Circulated amongst the Subscribers at least one week before the Annual General Meeting.

17.—That the Annual General Meeting of the Society shall be convened by public advertisement, at least one Month before Good Friday, stating the Time and Place where the Meeting will be held, to elect Officers, and to receive the Annual Report of the Committee, which shall contain a general Statement of Accounts, duly audited; the Rules and Progress of the Society, and an accurate List of Subscribers.

18.—That power be given to the Committee to render Pecuniary Assistance, at the expense of the Society, to deserving Members in distress.

19.—That none of the Rules herein contained shall be rescinded, or altered, or new ones made except at the Annual General Meeting of the Society; and that any Member or Members wishing to introduce any *new* Rules or Regulations, he or they must give notice of the same, in writing, to the Secretary, at least one week previous to the Annual General Meeting; and that none of the Rules or Alterations shall be binding until confirmed at the Annual General Meeting of the Society.

20.—That all the Rules and Regulations affecting the Cumberland and Westmoreland Wrestling Society heretofore existing shall be null and void; and that the present Rules and Regulations shall be the governing Rules of the Society.

www.ingramcontent.com/pod-product-compliance
Lightning Source LLC
Chambersburg PA
CBHW030312270326
41926CB00010B/1333